THE C2C & REIVERS
COMPLETE GUIDE

By Mark Porter

Accommodation, food and drink,
history, route and maps

11th Edition

C2C & Reivers Complete Guide
11th Edition

Copyright: Baytree Press

Published by Baytree Press
Albert House
Townfoot, Rothbury,
Northumberland,
NE65 7SR
Tel: 07767 893790
Email: mark@baytreepress.com
Website: www.baytreepress.com

ISBN 0-9544827-5-1

Distributed by: Cordee Books & Maps
3a de Montfort St
Leicester
LE1 7HD
Tel: 0116 254 3579
www.cordee.co.uk
sales@cordee.co.uk

C2C CYCLE ROUTE

PART I – C2C

A: WHITEHAVEN 22
– beginning of C2C and end of Reivers.
Taking a) the route to Keswick - via Loweswater, Lorton 28
and Whinlatter. Or...

B: WORKINGTON 31
- taking b) the route to Keswick via Wordsworth's Cockermouth and the
shores of Bassenthwaite Lake. Either way, both routes go through...

REIVERS CYCLE ROUTE

INTRODUCTION

This year is the eleventh anniversary of Britain's most popular and best known cycle route and this guide has just been updated to give you the very latest news, information and accommodation details.

The route is also going from strength to strength. In recent years, some 12–13,000 riders annually have been tackling it. 2003, with its Indian summer, attracted even more than before, though figures at the time of going to press were not available for 2004. However, last year's unremittingly dismal summer is likely to have impacted negatively on that total so if B&B owners and hoteliers noticed a drop in numbers, that probably explains it.

There is something about propelling oneself from one side of Britain to the other which captures the imagination. It is an easily quantifiable achievement – just like Land's End to John O'Groats, but on a much more manageable scale.

It combines the majestic beauty of the Northern Lakes, whose unspoilt charms are much the same as they would have been in Wordsworth's day, with the beauty of the Eden valley, and the challenge of the Pennines. Then the route crosses bleak tracts of post-industrial heritage before entering Newcastle and Sunderland. This epic journey has everything you could want on a route which holds appeal to expert and beginner alike, and can be managed over a long weekend.

The route was set up by the sustainable transport charity Sustrans and this guide is designed to be used with the Sustrans C2C Map obtainable from the Sustrans online shop or mail order line - visit www.sustrans.org.uk or call 0845 113 0065.

The C2C forms part of the National Cycle Network, which is a comprehensive network of safe and attractive routes for cycling and walking throughout the UK. A total of 10,000 miles will have been completed in September 2005, one third of which will be on traffic-free paths; the rest will follow quiet lanes or traffic-calmed roads. It is delivered through the policies and programmes of over 450 local authorities and other partners and is co-ordinated by Sustrans.

As for the Reivers Route, which will take you back to your starting point via some spectacular and remote countryside, an excellent map is available from Footprint, Unit 87, Stirling Enterprise Park, Stirling, FK7 7RP, 01786 479886 or www.footprintmaps.co.uk. They have kindly allowed us to reproduce some of their mapping plus map profiles which allow you to assess the hilly bits.

Your hosts have all been chosen for their understanding of the cyclist's needs, a warm welcome, acceptance of muddy legs, a secure place for your bike and provision of a meal either with them or at a nearby pub.

The C2C is designed to be tackled west to east to take advantage of the prevailing winds. Both the Sustrans map and this accommodation guide run from west to east, while the return leg along the Reivers – for those brave enough to tackle the whole circuit – was tailor-made for an east-west crossing of the UK.

Please try to book accommodation, meals and packed lunches in advance, and do not arrive unannounced expecting beds and meals to be available. If you have to cancel a booking, please give the proprietor as much notice as you can so that the accommodation can be re-let. Your deposit may be forfeited: this is at the discretion of the proprietor.

Suggestions for additional addresses are most welcome, together with your comments. We are particularly keen to receive reports about the efficacy of waymarking on both routes, and comments (both positive and adverse) on our route tips and guidance.

Please note: the information given in the Guide was correct at the time of printing and was as supplied by the proprietors. No responsibility can be accepted by this independent B&B guide as to completeness or accuracy, nor for any loss arising as a result. It is advisable to check the relevant details when booking.

JOHN NAYLOR: We are deeply sorry to note the sudden death in February of John Naylor, one of the guiding hands behind the route. John was largely repsonsible for the first 10 miles out of Whitehaven as well as the spectacular boardwalk from Keswick - a fitting and lasting testament to a talented builder and designer who served the charity Groundwork West Cumbria for many years. John, who leaves behind a young family, will be sorely missed.

FOREWORD

The C2C ride has been a memorable experience for over 100,000 cyclists over the last 10 years - an achievable challenge, a memorable ride, wonderful scenery, and so often excellent hospitality along the way. When you arrive wet and exhausted, nothing matters quite so much as the welcome you receive, a place to put your bike, somewhere to dry your clothes and a hot bath! Somehow these routines of everyday life become so much more important on a journey like the C2C.

This guide can promise you just this welcome so that staying overnight along the route is just as memorable as the journey itself. At the same time, your expenditure is supporting the local economy with so far over £15 million spread out over the length of the route, which has taken more than its fair share of knocks over the last few years.

By cycling you do more than support just local businesses, you demonstrate that the tourist industry can touch lightly on the beautiful countryside we all flock to see, that it isn't necessary to drive for this pleasure, and that you have made your own personal contribution towards a sustainable future for the stressed out planet we all share.

I hope that inspired by this trip you will cycle more - there is the whole 10,000 miles of the National Cycle Network to start with!

John Grimshaw, MBE
Founder and Chief Executive
Sustrans

ACKNOWLEDGEMENTS

Many thanks to David Gray, the Sustrans man in Stanley, Co Durham. He was instrumental in putting together the C2C, along with John Grimshaw and the late John Naylor.

Some of their images have been reproduced in the following pages, along with Martin Herron, Julia Bayne, Barry Wilson, Pat Strachan, G.L. Jones and Steve Morgan.

Newcastle Gateshead Initiative, the Cumbria Tourist Board picture library and Ben Barden, Footprint Maps for their co-operation with the splendid Reivers route, and www.thecumbriadirectory.com, whose excellent website provided useful background information.

Sustrans is the UK's leading sustainable transport charity and works on practical projects to encourage people to walk, cycle and use public transport to benefit health and the environment. Their flagship project is the award winning National Cycle Network. Sustrans' work relies on the generous donations and monthly standing orders of supporters and the support of charitable trusts, companies and the National Lottery. If you enjoy the C2C, why not become a Sustrans supporter?

For more details, call 0845 113 0065 or visit: www.sustrans.org.uk.

The picture below, taken in 1994, shows the team who built the C2C.

9

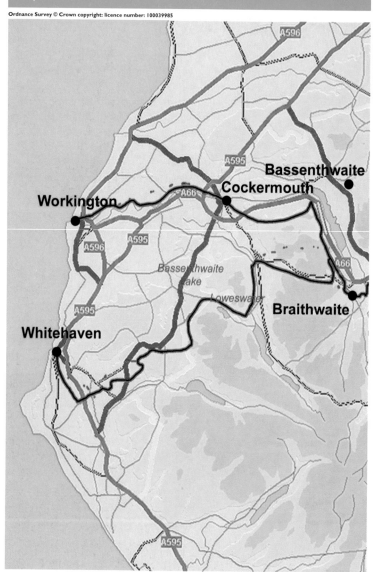

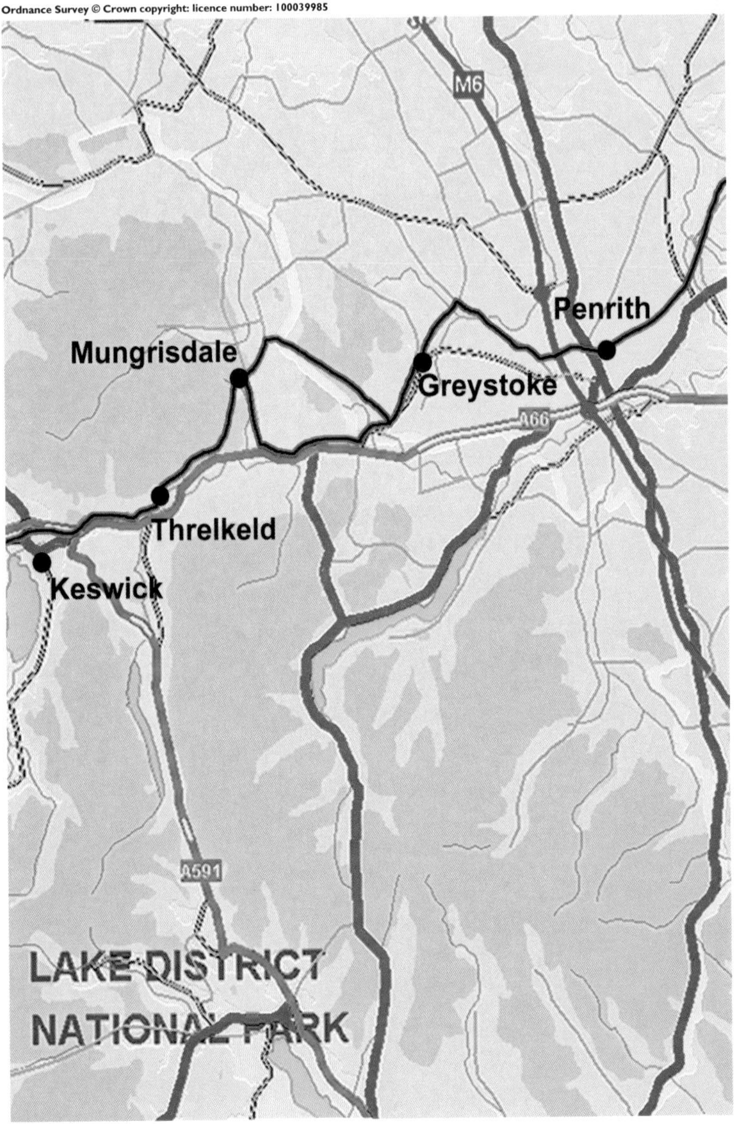
M6
Penrith
Mungrisdale
Greystoke
A66
Threlkeld
Keswick
A591
LAKE DISTRICT
NATIONAL PARK

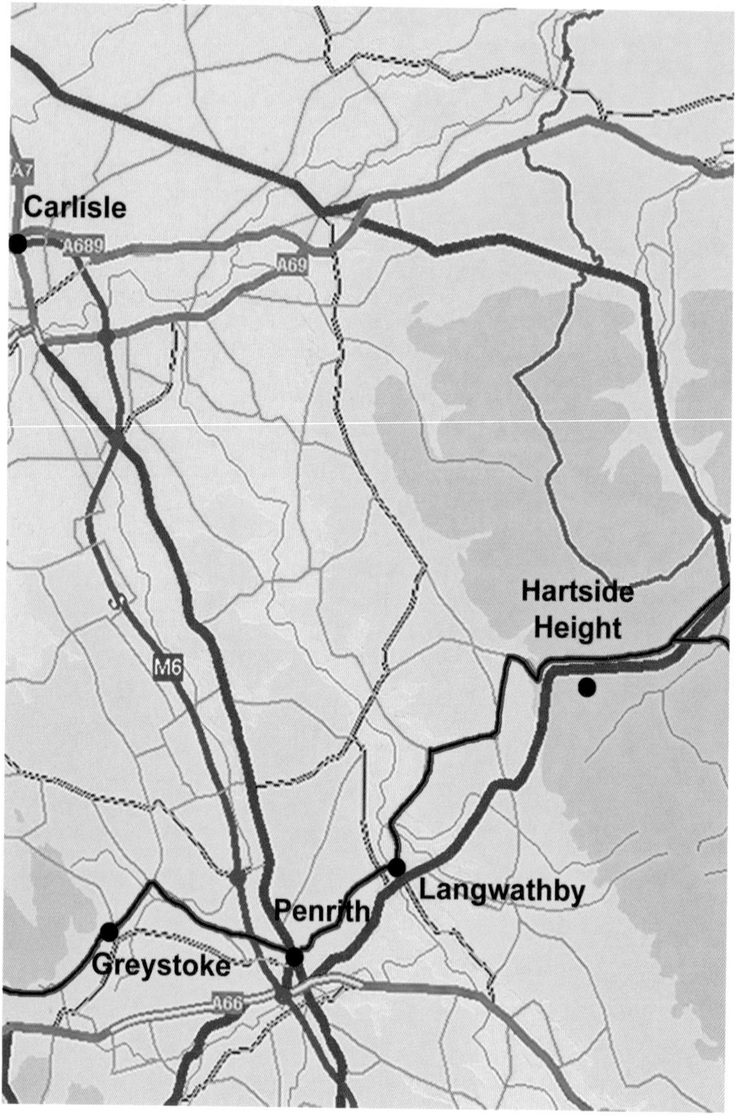
A7
Carlisle
A689
A69
M6
Hartside
Height
Langwathby
Penrith
Greystoke
A66

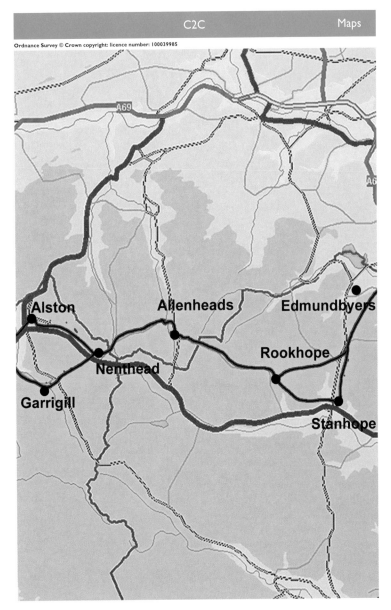

Ordnance Survey © Crown copyright: licence number: 100039985

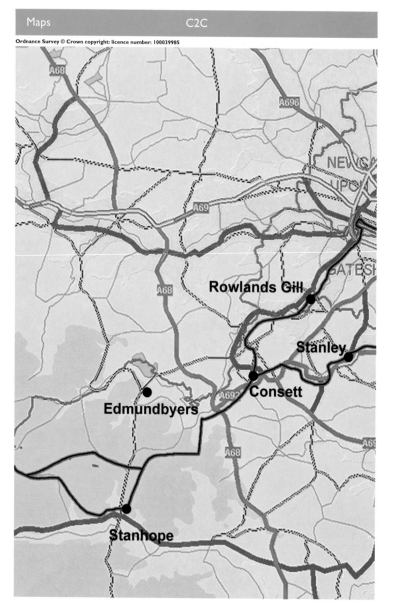

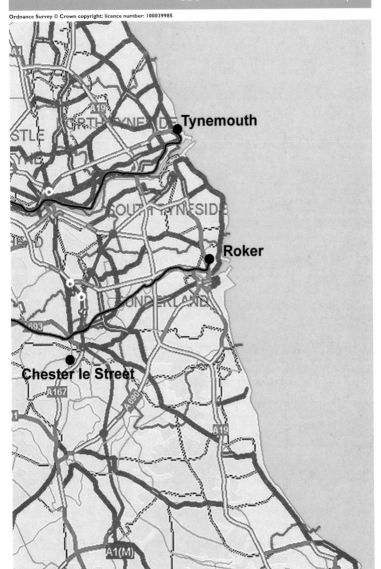

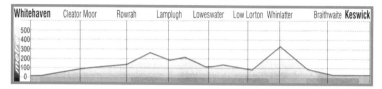

Whitehaven - Keswick: 49.6km (31 miles) 19.2km of which are traffic-free.
Quiet country lanes and railway paths.

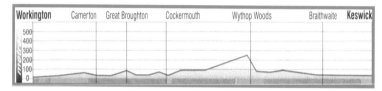

Workington - Keswick: 38.4km (24 miles) 8km of which are traffic-free. Old
industrial start into quiet countryside, lakes and lanes.

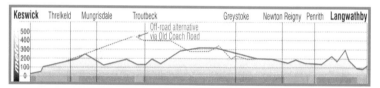

Keswick - Langwathby: 45km (28 miles) 10km of which are traffic-free. Easy
ride through the Eden valley. You can make it hard by taking the Coach Road.

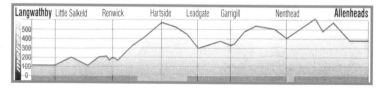

Langwathby - Allenheads: 45km (28 miles). All on minor roads. Four big hills
within 30km - the hardest section.

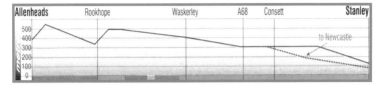

Allenheads - Stanley: 51km (32 miles), of which 26km are traffic-free. Couple of stinkers to start an otherwise downhill day.

Stanley - Sunderland, Roker: 26km (16 miles), of which 22.4 are traffic-free. Enjoy the gentle roll in along the river.

Rowlands Gill - Tynemouth: 30 km (19 miles), of which 27.2 are traffic-free. Glorious municipal end to a wild rural ride.

Route profiles reproduced with permission from
SUSTRANS. www.sustrans.org.uk

B&B ABBREVIATIONS

You can assume that accommodation is non-smoking unless otherwise specified. Similarly, drying facilities and secure storage for bikes are provided. Most of the rooms are en-suite but are only marked as such if the proprietor specifies. Accommodation is on or very close to the route unless otherwise specified.

R=Rooms; S=Single; D=Double;
T=Twin; F=Family; Tpl=Triple; B=Bunks
E=Email; W=Website;
EM=Evening Meal; PL=Packed Lunch;
SP=Smoking Permitted;
DFR=Distance From Route
E-S=En-Suite
<=from/more than

All establishments have been chosen not only for their cycle friendliness, but other considerations as having drying facilities and secure storage for bikes.

WAY MARKING

The route is waymarked with a blue direction sign complete with the letters C2C and a red number 7 – the number of the route. These are posted at junctions and other strategic spots. Occasionally the road surface is signed; sometimes there are just little plastic stickers posted to gates and lamp-posts. Signage is not always brilliant, but with sharp eyes and the use of a map you should not get lost. Having said that, sections at the beginning and end are notorious for lack of signs; vandals like to trash them and souvenir hunters snaffle them.

MAPS

There is basic mapping in this guide, along with topographical maps showing profiles of such beastly climbs as Hartside. You will also need the Sustrans C2C map. If you want to take Ordnance Survey Landranger, you will need numbers 89,90, 86,87,88. But this will be very bulky and unnecessary in view of the waymarking. You can, of course, invest in the OS Interactive Atlas, and download the relevant sections. This two CD option was around £30.

WHERE TO START AND HOW TO GET THERE

The C2C is designed to be cycled from west coast to east coast. This is because of prevailing winds and gradients: do it this way and, god-willing, the wind will be behind you and most of the climbs will be short and sharp, rather than long and grinding. East to west, therefore, is for those who like unrelentingly hostile gradients with the wind in their face. If you want to cycle east to west, a more user-friendly route is the Reivers (see p. 107)

TRAIN

There are two choices of start, just as there are two choices of finish. Let's start at the start: Whitehaven or Workington? These two ports are accessible by train if you take the local First North Western line from Carlisle. The journey takes about an hour, following the dramatic and spectacular coastline. If opting for the train, remember to book your bike on in advance.

National Rail Enquiries: 08457 484950
First North Western: 08457 000125 (sales); 08456 001159 (customer services).
Virgin Trains (who run the west coast service): 08457 222333.

AIR

Newcastle Airport is only 20 minutes from the city centre and there are regular and frequent links to many European cities, including Amsterdam, Brussels and Paris, along with international connections to the rest of the world. There are also direct flights to Aberdeen, Birmingham, Gatwick, Heathrow, Wick, Dublin and Belfast.
T: 0191 286 0966
E: www.newcastleairport.com

SEA

The International Ferry Terminal at Royal Quays is the North of England's main sea link with Scandinavia and Continental Europe and operates regular passenger services from Norway, Sweden and the Netherlands. It is an ideal start point for the Reivers, Hadrian's Wall or C2C in reverse if you don't fancy getting the train across to Whitehaven or Workington.

Fjordline T: 0191 296 1313
DFDS Seaways T: 0191 293 6262

When returning to Whitehaven or Workington from Sunderland or Tynemouth, you will have to make your way to Newcastle Central station to get the train across to Carlisle. I have heard many reports of local rail services being unhelpful to cyclists. There has, I gather, been a big change in attitude in the last couple of years and they are altogether more helpful – though this is at the discretion of the guard or ticket inspector.

Motorised alternatives in the form of specialist taxi services, some of whom will organise the whole package for you, are readily available for the return journey.

Holiday Lakeland, nr Keswick: 016973 71871 (*see inside back cover*).
Tyne Valley Holidays, Newcastle: 0191 284 7534 (*see p. 162*)
The Bike Bus, Stanley Mini Coaches, Stanley: 01207 237424 (*see p.166*)
Discovery Travel: 01904 766564 (*see p. 167*)

If you are coming by car most accommodation owners will allow you to leave your vehicle with them. Or you may prefer a secure long-term car park. There is one in the centre of Whitehaven. For further information call the Tourist Information Centre:

Whitehaven: 01946 852939
Workington: 01900 606699

There is also £3 a day parking one mile from the start of the C2C at one of the last mile points on the home leg of the Reivers Route, run by a Sustrans ranger, no less (contact Jim Hewitson on 01946 692178). In Workington, there's parking at the quayside for £2.50 a day (contact

Martin Perkins 01900 604997).

Back-up vehicles are kindly requested to use main roads in order to keep the C2C as traffic-free as possible.

A. WHITEHAVEN

Whitehaven has the distinction of being the start of the C2C and the finish of the Reivers routes. It may not be quite the place it was in the 18th century, when it played a significant role in the British slave industry and was the main importer of tobacco on the west coast. Nonetheless it has undergone a major transformation in the last couple of years, its fine Georgian architecture now looking spruce and proud.

Perhaps the most impressive feature is the large harbour, which has undergone a £68 million facelift. There is a fine 100-berth marina, now choc-a-bloc with pleasure craft of all sizes and shapes. The town has, in short, reacquired some of the prosperity it lost in the years after it became the world's first new town.

Not so long ago it would have been hard to imagine that early Manhattan's street grid system was based on the pattern the Lowther family laid out for Whitehaven in the late 1690s, when it became apparent that the Cumbrian settlement was destined for great things.

Shortly afterwards the streets filled with rum and sugar merchants, slave traders and tobacco speculators and America-bound settlers waiting for their boat to come in. The harbour was teeming with coal transporters, which plied the Irish Sea to supply Dublin's houses and industries with black stuff dynamited from under Whitehaven's seabed. There was also shipbuilding; over 1,000 vessels were built in the Whitehaven yards, and one of the oldest surviving iron-built ships was constructed here. After London and Bristol, this was the third busiest port in England.

Connections with America went deep: John Paul Jones, founder of the American navy and erstwhile scourge of Britain's own, gained his sea legs as a merchant seaman from Whitehaven. Indeed, the last invasion of the English mainland, in 1778, was perpetrated by

Jones upon the town. The incursion was part of the only ever attack on British soil by US forces; and we should not forget that George Washington's granny, Mildred Warner Gale, lived here and is buried at St Nicholas's churchyard.

The town has been impressively preserved, one suspects, because a sudden lack of prosperity after the boom years disinclined planners from bulldozing in the name of progress. This left the Lowther architectural heritage preserved, as it were, in aspic. It is worthwhile walking the streets, admiring this memorial to an earlier and prosperous age, when sea captains and merchants lived in style.

There are many interesting and quirky sculptures around the harbour, street mosaics featuring different aspects of the heritage, plus a mural in Washington Square and a plethora of shiny plaques above doorways giving a clue to the past.

It is one of my favourite places on the whole route and it seems a shame just to use Whitehaven as a point of departure without spending the previous night exploring. There are plenty of distractions, in the form of pubs, restaurants and venues. The following day's ride out of this port is nothing if not leisurely – a stark contrast to the undulations that are to follow. A late night is not going to spoil it.

The traditional way to start this route is by christening your bike on the slipway behind the big C2C sign by dipping the front wheel in the briny. Then you might wish to get your first route stamp at the New Espresso café in the Market Place.

Just out of Whitehaven: seat with a view.

WHERE TO EAT

American Connection - Marlborough Street - 01946 693671
Zest Restaurant: Harbourside - 01946 66981
Georgian House - Church Street - 01946 696611
Casa Romana [Italian] - Queen Street - 01946 591901
Jasmine Palace, [Chinese/Thai] Duke/Strand Street.
Blue Wine Bar & Restaurant - Tangier Street - 01946 691986
Hornblowers - Church Street - 01946 590492
Westminster Restaurant - Lowther Street - 01946 694404
Askash Tandoori Restaurant [Indian] - 01946 691171
Ali Taj Restaurant [Indian] - 01946 592679
Golden Harbour [Chinese] - George Street - 01946 693388
Howgate Brewster & Travel Inn - Howgate - 01946 66286

PLACES OF INTEREST

Michael Moon's, Bookshop & Gallery, Roper St. One of the largest bookshops in Cumbria, "vast and gloriously eccentric!"

The Beacon: Local maritime and industrial history within the Harbour Gallery. 01946 592302.

The Rum Story, exhibition celebrating the Jefferson family business, the oldest booze empire in Britain.

The Haig Mining Museum, Haig Enterprise Park, High Rd.

CYCLE SHOPS

Haven Cycles: Cycle Hire/Repairs, Preston St Garage 01946 632 633 (see p.164).

Dave Milling, Preston St. 01946 63380

MORESBY HALL, Jane & David Saxon,
Moresby, Whitehaven CA28 6PJ.
T: 01946 696317
E: c2c@moresbyhall.co.uk
W: www.moresbyhall.co.uk

R: 2D, 2T, 1F + 2 cottages to sleep 6.
B&B: £35 - £60 EM: £22 (please book ahead).
PL: £5. Pub or restaurant: 500m.
ETC 4 diamonds + Silver Award.
Grade I listed country house with spacious well equipped en-suite rooms.
Great architectural and historical interest. Superb breakfasts using local
produce, fully licensed and warm welcome from owners Jane and David.

ALVA HOUSE B&B, Mrs Kathy Cunliffe,
nr. Moor Row,
Whitehaven, Cumbria CA24 3SX
T: 01946 814537
E: CunliffeK@aol.com
W: www.alva-house.com.

R: 2D, 1T, 1F (E-S). B&B: £23 - £28
EM: £10 - £12. PL: £3.50. Pub nearby
Secluded Edwardian family home bang on the C2C. En suite rooms, tea/
coffee making facilities and TV. Secure bike storage, fell views and warm
welcome. Parking and secure cycle storage.

WAVERLEY HOTEL, Cheryl Twinn,
Tangier Street, Whitehaven, CA28 7UX.
T: 01946 694 337
F: 01946 691 577
E: waverleyhotel@amserve.net
W: www.waverleyhotel.co.uk
R: 10S, 5D, 6T, 3F.
B&B: £24.50 - £45
EM: £3.95-£10.95. PL: £4.95. SP. DFR: 50m.
Licensed restaurant. Privately owned hotel. Town centre location. Close to
habourside.

THE CROSS GEORGIAN GUEST HOUSE,
Joyce Bailey,
Sneckyeat Rd,
Hensingham,
Whitehaven
CA28 8JQ.
T: 01946 63716

E: thecross.guesthouse@virgin.net
R: ID, 3F (happy to let as singles)
B&B: £17 - £25. EM: No. PL: £3.50. SP.
Near pubs and eating places. Close to route and 3km from town centre.
Locally inspected. Family run Grade II listed Georgian gem in a quiet out-of-town location with ample parking. Breakfast and vegetarian choices.
Panoramic views.

THE MANSION, T. Todd, Old Woodhouse,
Whitehaven, CA28 9LN.
T/F: 01946 61860/691270. E: comnenus4@aol.com
R: 12 D. B&B: £14.00 - £20.
EM: £6.00-£7.50 PL: £3.50.
DFR: 1 km.
Friendly, relaxed and with all mod cons. Super big screen TV and swimming pool.

WHITEHAVEN, EGREMONT

BOOKWELL GARTH GUEST HOUSE,
Wayne & Jeannette Powell,
16 Bookwell, Egremont, CA22 2LS.
T: 01946 820 271
R: 5S, 7T. B&B: £18-£19. EM: no. PL: £3.50.
DFR: 1.5km. Pub 150m.
Friendly Guest House with good accommodation, TV in all rooms. Drying facilities, good location. Early breakfast.

C2C underpass on the Whitehaven-Rowrah railway path

As you leave Whitehaven harbour you will join the Whitehaven-Rowrah cycle path which links the sea to the fells. But first some detailed instructions for getting onto the route proper: out of the harbour head right up Quay St, then left past the Tourist Information Centre through Market Place and into Preston St. Look out for signs off to the left for the path which goes behind Focus DIY and then onto Esk Avenue, only to rejoin the path by the school. You then cycle along Croasdale Av and Wasdale Av before linking up with the path to exit the town.

You now follow the railway line built in the 1850s to carry limestone, coal and iron; it is now a sculpture trail interpreting the geology and industrial history of the region. You might find yourself stopping to check signage; this is fairly routine, as there are several other routes around here.

The rail line goes as far as Rowrah in the direction of Kirkland. Just beyond Rowrah turn left onto the lane and right at the school. You will soon pass Felldyke and, following signs for Loweswater, Lamplugh.

In about 5km you will be skirting Loweswater, your first glimpse of the Lakes and a wonderful spot to take pictures or stop for a snack. Beyond the lake is the picturesque village of Loweswater, complete with church and village inn; a delightful place to stop if you're really taking your time, or are on foot.

From Loweswater continue up the lane through Thackthwaite and soon you will cross the River Cocker at Low Lorton, passing through Lorton Vale and into High Lorton. This is a truly picturesque Northern Lakes village to spend a night.

LORTON

Wainwright, Britain's most famous walking hero and al fresco author, regarded this area, with its deeply gouged valleys reached from the passes of Whinlatter, Honister and Newlands, as his favourite spot.

Lorton is only about 5km from Cockermouth, so is an optional stop-off for those departing from Workington.

WINDER HALL COUNTRY HOUSE,
Ann and Nick Lawler,
Low Lorton, Cockermouth,
Cumbria CA13 9UP
T: 01900 85107 F: 01900 85479
E: nick@winderhall.co.uk
W: www.winderhall.co.uk
R: 7D, 2T, 2F, 2
Four-posters (E-S)
B&B: £45-£55. EM: £25. PL: £4
DFR: 100m   Pub 100yds
5 Diamonds + Fine Dining Award.
Beautiful hide-away location in a historical manor house just off C2C. Pamper yourself after a hard day in the saddle with luxurious food and gorgeous rooms.

MEADOW BANK
Christine Edmunds,
High Lorton,
Cockermouth,
CA13 9UG
T/F: 01900 85315
E: CEdm85315@aol.com
W: www.buttermerecumbria.com
R: 1D, 1T (E-S)
B&B: £20 - £22.
EM: no. PL: £3.50
DFR: 300m. Pub 1km.
A warm welcome awaits in this picturesque location.
Secure bike storage, drying facilities – pub close by.

To get to New House (below) on the B5289, you can either a) carry on straight through Loweswater for 3km on the road parallel with the route, or b) turn right onto the B5289 at the cross-roads just beyond the Lorton bridge. It's only 2km from the route.

NEW HOUSE FARM, Hazel Thompson,
Lorton, Nr Cockermouth, CA13 9UU
T: 01900 85404
F: 01900 85478
E: hazel@newhouse-farm.co.uk
W: www.newhouse-farm.co.uk
R: 5D, 1T (E-S)
B&B: £46 - £60
EM: £22-£24. PL: £7
DFR: 2km
Pub: 2km
5 Diamonds:

'Winning 17th century grade II listed farmhouse set in stunning surroundings. Beautiful antiques throughout compliment the original oak beams, flag floors and stone fireplaces where log fires crackle on colder days. Four posters, hot tub in the garden. Delicious food.'

The first real challenge comes when you leave High Lorton: the uphill slog to Whinlatter, the first section of which is fairly unremitting, until you join the B5292 on the Whinlatter Pass. Now you should bear right along the forest track, then first left along the wide track, ignoring other routes to off to the right. This path takes you over rough terrain for a couple of kilometres before coming out on the B5292 again, at which point go left then right for the Whinlatter Visitor Centre (if for any reason the off-road track is closed, as it was when I last cycled the C2C, then continue along the road to the visitor centre).

You are in the heart of England's only mountain forest. Because of the pure mountain air a sanatorium used to stand in the Whinlatter Forest. Sailors with TB and other communicable diseases were kept there in isolation.

Just beyond the visitor centre the route goes sharp right down a forest track to Thornthwaite. It commands some stunning views of Bassenthwaite Lake. Take time, weather permitting, to admire Blencathra, Skiddaw and, over to the right, Helvellyn.

There are plans for this whole area to have extensive mountain bike routes built, and for it to become a cycling 'hub' for the northern Lakes. Also take time to have a good look around the visitor centre. A must for ornithologists, it also contains a wealth of forest habitat information and has a fine tea room. At Thornthwaite the route links up with the Workington to Keswick alternative, via the Braithwaite and Portinscale, where there are some charming places to stay which I shall highlight after outlining the Workington route.

View towards Skiddaw path below Whinlatter

Cumbrian ports: the smoke-stacks are gone, but the memories are there

ALTERNATIVE START: B: WORKINGTON

European funding is being used to help restore this fine working town and there are high hopes that its resurgence will bring with it tourism and a new lease of life, as has happened in Whitehaven and Maryport, just up the coast. There is some fine Georgian architecture and some stunning industrial heritage.

Workington is an ancient market and industrial town at the mouth of the River Derwent. Parts of it date back to Roman times. But it was not until the 18th century, with the exploitation of local iron ore and coal that Workington expanded to become a major industrial town and port. In this respect its growth reflects that of its neighbour, Whitehaven, twelve kilometres down the coast.

Iron and steel manufacture have always been part of Workington's raison d'etre, and it was here that Henry Bessemer first introduced his revolutionary steel making process. In recent years, with the decline of the steel industry and coal mining, the town has diversified into other forms of industry.

Whilst not as pretty as Whitehaven, the advantage of starting here is that the opening leg of the journey is 11km shorter, has gentler gradients and passes through the beautiful market town of Cockermouth. It is also close to, and goes through, Camerton, where the church sits prettily on the banks of the Derwent and the splendidly named Black Tom Inn beckons passers-by.

It also has some nice churches. The parish church of St Michael's has stood on its present site since the 7th century, although the 12th century Norman church was replaced in 1770 by a larger building. Sadly this was severely damaged by fire in 1994, but has since undergone a major rebuilding programme. St John's Church was built in 1823 to commemorate the battle of Waterloo, to a design by Thomas Hardwick. It is built of local sandstone, and bears some resemblance to Inigo Jones' St. Paul's Church in Covent Garden, London.

PLACES OF INTEREST

The Helena Thompson Museum was bequeathed to the people of Workington by the eponymous Miss Thompson, a local philanthropist, in 1940. It houses displays of pottery, silver, glass, and furniture dating from Georgian times, as well as the social and industrial history of Workington and the surrounding area.

Workington Hall is built around a pele tower dating from the 14th century, and was once one of the finest Manor houses in the region. This striking ruin, once owned by the Curwen family, Lords of the Manor of Workington, gave shelter to Mary Queen of Scots on her last flight from Scotland before her imprisonment and execution. Apparently it is haunted by Henry Curwen.

Jane Pit is a 19th century coal mine built by Henry Curwen, and the remains of this can be seen at Mossbay.

WHERE TO EAT

Impressions, 173 Vulcans Lane: traditional English food 01900 605 446
Super Fish, 20 Pow St: sit-in or takeaway 01900 604 916
Blue Dolphin, 1 Lismore Pl: sit-in or t-away 01900 604114
The Carnegie Colours, Finkle St: home-cooking 01900 605743
Treats, 26 Finkle St: good cafe 01900 871752
The Old Townhouse, Portland Sq: upmarket 01900 871332 **(see B&B entry opposite)**

CYCLE SHOPS

Bike Bank 18-20 Market Place 01900 603 337
Halfords, Derwent Howe Retail Park 01900 601635

Workington Tourist Information Centre: 01900 606699

MORVEN HOUSE HOTEL,
Mrs Caroline Nelson,
Siddick Road,
Workington, Cumbria, CA14 1LE USE
T/F: 01900 602118
E: cnelsonmorven@aol.com.
W: www.morvenguesthouse.gbr.cc
R: 2S, 2D, 5T (SP some rooms).
B&B: £22-£27. EM: £10-£12. PL: £4.50. Pub On site. 3 Diamonds. A relaxed, informal atmosphere, an ideal stopover for C2C/Reivers participants near start. Car park and very secure cycle storage. *(SEE AD ON PAGE 163)*

WAVERLEY HOTEL,
Lynn Pears, Gordon St,
Workington CA14 2EN
T: 01900 603246 F: 01900 604745
E: sales@waverley-hotel.com
W: www.waverley-hotel.com
B&B: £20 - £28. DB&B: £27 - £35
EM: £7 for 3 courses. PL: £3.50
Rooms: 6S, 8D, 10T, 1F. In town centre amongst pubs & restaurants. Friendly atmosphere and good food. We welcome cyclists and walkers and provide relevant information and maps.

THE OLD TOWNHOUSE,
Tim Dalby,
3 Portland St,
Workington CA14 4BQ
T & F: 01900 871332
W: www.theoldtownhouse.com
R: 1S, 1D, 1T, 1F
B&B: charges per room from £30.
EM:
Townhouse has a fine restaurant with 2 AA Rosettes. B&B has just started up in this 500 year old building, tucked away in the most historic part of town. Just 100m from the centre, there are lots of pubs nearby.

The route starts from the lighthouse. You get there by turning down Curwen Rd on the industrial estate.

From the lighthouse turn left onto the railway bridge just by the sailing club, then (briefly) follow the path by the side of the river Derwent. Bear left at the next railway bridge, crossing the line at the road junction, where you turn right. At the main road go right and under the sandstone bridge where you meet the walkway / cycle path which then bears left, heading out of the industrial part of Workington past the lagoon and up through Seaton.

Follow the route through Camerton, briefly joining the river again, skirting Broughton Moor and on through Great Broughton and Papcastle, once the site of a Roman fort. You are now on the edge of Cockermouth.

Historic Cockermouth: Wordsworth was here

COCKERMOUTH

One of the most attractive towns in the North West, Cockermouth is one of only two places in the Lake District to be designated a 'Gem Town' by the Department of the Environment, some 40 years ago. That means it is protected and must remain the same in perpetuity.

It lies just outside the boundary of the Lake District National Park and perhaps for this reason is not inundated with tourists and all the tackiness that often goes with the industry.

The town received its Market Charter in 1221, and has retained its importance as a market town ever since. Quarrying and mining for lead and iron were later developments outside the town, and a brewery has been built at the foot of the castle mound, where the two rivers meet.

It has long held a fascination for writers, poets and artists and is the birthplace of William and Dorothy Wordsworth. One of the finest buildings in Cockermouth is Wordsworth House, the Lakeland poet's family home, now in the care of the National Trust.

The great architectural guru Sir Nikolaus Pevsner in his 'Buildings of England', described the place as 'quite a swagger house for such a town'. Built in 1745 for the then High Sheriff of Cumberland, Joshua Lucock, it was bought in 1761 by Sir James Lowther, son of Sir John, who built Whitehaven and its port. John Wordsworth, the poet's father, moved to Cockermouth as agent to Sir James in 1764, and in 1766 married and moved into what is now known as Wordsworth House. Here four sons and a daughter were born. Their mother died when William was eight, and he went to live with relations in Penrith.

The house thrived as a private residence until 1937, when it was put on the market. A prime location in the centre of town, bosses of the local bus company saw their chance and snapped it up. It was the natural spot for a new bus station, so they applied for – and got – planning permission to bulldoze it.

However there was such a national outcry that sufficient funds were raised from far and wide for the town to buy it back. It was promptly handed over to the National Trust repetition. The old kitchen and housekeeper's room now serve as a café/restaurant where you can get morning coffee, light lunches and afternoon tea.

Two other famous locals came from Eaglesfield, a mile from the town's centre, were born within two years of each other: Fletcher Christian, the man who led the mutiny on 'The Bounty' was born in 1764, and attended the same school as Wordsworth; and two years later John Dalton, who was one of the most brilliant scientists of his age, and was the originator of the atomic theory.

Cockermouth Castle was built in the 13th century, but little of that remains because of the efforts of Robert the Bruce. The majority of today's ruins date from 1360 to 1370.

PLACES OF INTEREST

The Museum of Printing (01900 824984) has a varied and fascinating range of printing presses brought together from all over Britain.
Castlegate House (01900 822149) contemporary art exhibitions.
The Toy and Model Museum: mainly British toys from 1900 onwards.
Jennings Brewery offers 1.5 hour tours around the Brewery, explaining the various processes involved in brewing traditional beer.
The Bitter End is the first pub in Cumbria to have its own working brewery - 'Cumbria's Smallest Brewery'.
Lakeland Sheep and Wool Centre at the nearby roundabout on the A66, is where you can meet Cumbria's most famous residents.
Western Lake District Visitor Centre - all about the area.
Tourist Information Centre is at the Town Hall, Market Place, Cockermouth, CA13 9NP (Tel: 01900 822634).

WHERE TO EAT

Beatfords Country Restaurant, 01900 827099 7, Lowther Went South St.
Cheers Bistro, 01900 822109 22, Main St.
Junipers Restaurant & Cafe Bar 01900 822892 11 South St.
Norham Coffee House & Restaurant, 01900 824330 73 Main St.
Nikki's Italian Restaurant, 01900 821223 7 Old Kings Arms Lane.
Quince & Medlar Fine Food, 01900 823579 13 Castlegate. (Vegetarian)
Taste of India, 01900 827844 4-5 Headford Court, Main St.
The Bitter End Brew Pub, 01900 828993 15 Kirkgate.
Lee's Chinese Takeaway & Fish and Chips, 01900 827770 47 Main St.
Cross over Gote St from the Papcastle road and continue past the

James Walker factory, then right onto Bridge St, crossing the river just after the doctor's surgery.

You then head left onto Main St. Go past Station St before turning right into Challoner St, left into Cocker Lane and then almost immediately right to follow the river, under Lorton St towards the Youth Hostel, before turning right to swivel over the river Cocker and follow the path past the cemetery before the hairpin right turn onto Strawberry Home Rd, where you take a left. It is now a straightforward run.

You may wish to stop off near the shores of Bassenthwaite's northern tip, in which case go through the village of Wythop Mill and turn right by the phone box. Turn left at the Pheasant Inn and go over the A66 onto the B5291, taking the scenic Ouse Bridge to the Castle Inn Hotel *(see page160-1)*. It's a short hop up to the village and the Sun Inn, where they serve good food and ale.

Assuming you do not opt for this diversion, you will encounter a short, hilly section before the descent to Bassenthwaite Lake, from whence it is an easy ride into Keswick. At Thornthwaite you meet up with the Whitehaven route.

Bassenthwaite Lake seen from Thornthwaite

ROSE COTTAGE, John and Susan Graham,
Lorton Road, Cockermouth, Cumbria
CA13 9DX
T/F: 01900 822 189
E: bookings@rosecottageguest.co.uk
W: www.rosecottageguest.co.uk
R: 4D, 3T, 2F, 1S

B&B: £27.50 - £45 EM: £18-£20. PL: from £6
DFR: 400m. Pub 500m. 4 Diamonds: A family run guest house in its own
grounds. All rooms en-suite with colour TV, tea/coffee, central heating and
most are double glazed. Warm friendly atmosphere.

RIVERSIDE B&B,
Rachel & Jean Habgood,
12 Market St,
Cockermouth CA13 9NJ
T: 01900 827504
R: 2T, 1S. B&B: £20-£22
EM: no. PL: £3.50 (prior notice, please) Friendly,
family run Georgian home with comfortable beds,

excellent breakfasts, local amenities nearby, tea-trays, fires and drying
facilities plus bike lock-up. Welcome!

STRATHEARN GUEST HOUSE,
6 Castlegate, Cockermouth,
Cumbria, CA13 9EU
T/F: 01900 826 749
E: waters.boyle@virgin.net
W: www.smoothhound.co.uk
R: 1S, 5D, 3T, 2F (4R E-S)
B&B £17.50-£25 EM: no.
PL: £5 (prior notice please).
Pub100m. Grade II listed Georgian townhouse. Full English,
vegetarian, continental breakfasts. H&C, tea/coffee, colour
TV in all rooms. Changing ownership as we went to press.

THORNTHWAITE

There is a Viking burial ground here at Powter Howe (see accommodation below) and just behind it is a hill called Barf. You will see two large white rocks – one half-way up Barf, and one at the bottom. The higher one is called The Bishop, and the lower one The Clerk. They commemorate a deadly drinking session back in the 18th century at the Swan Inn (recently transformed into holiday apartments) during which the bibulous Bishop of Londonderry, doubtless across on diocesan duty, bet his clerk that he could beat him to the top of Barf. With that, they downed their glasses and set off. The Right Reverend keeled over and died half-way up, and the clerk pegged it at the bottom, and the stones are said to commemorate this foolhardy wager. I do not know whether they were on their way up, or on their way down. Informed readers are welcome to write in.

Thornthwaite overlooks Bassenthwaite Lake. Bassenthwaite is the only lake in the Lake District. This may seem strange, but all the other large expanses of H2O in the so-called Lake District are called either 'Water' or 'Tarn'. The view below looks up towards Barf.

POWTER HOWE, Nimrod Lockwood,
Thornthwaite, Keswick, Cumbria CA12 5SQ
T/F: 017687 78415
R: 2D, 1T
B&B: £20-£25. EM: no. PL: £3.50
Pub 3km.
Sixteenth century farmhouse of great   character with magnificent
views over Bassenthwaite Lake towards Skiddaw. Set in two acres of
mature garden.

BRAITHWAITE

Just 3km down the road, nestling at the bottom of the Whinlatter
Pass and Newlands valley with the spectacular backdrop of Grisedale
Pike and Bassenthwaite Lake, is the picturesque village of Braithwaite.
Braithwaite is half-way between Thornthwaite and Keswick. It
makes an excellent base for touring the Lake District, and is close to
Loweswater, Crummock Water and Buttermere.

It's a straight and pleasant run through a quintessentially English
village scene, over a Medieval humped-back bridge. This section of
Braithwaite, leading out towards Little Braithwaite and Ullock, is
somehow preserved in time. Only cars spoil the scene – otherwise
you could be back in the 18th century. The route to Keswick via
Portinscale is well sign-posted. You come into Keswick up the main
street, following the traffic around to the left and up to the lights at the
Penrith Road. If not stopping in this delightful town, then go left down
Station St.

ROYAL OAK,
T & P Inns,
Terry Franks,
Braithwaite, Keswick,
CA12 5SY
T: 017687 78533.
E: tpfranks@hotmail.com
W: www.royaloak-braithwaite.co.uk
R: 1S, 6D, 2T, 1F. B&B: £30-£37.
EM: £7-£13. PL: £5
SP: not in restaurant.
AA 4 diamonds.

Country inn with rooms ideally located in the heart of the Lake District.
Sky TV. Fine local ales. Good food. Does gastro fare at the Farmers Arms
in nearby Portinscale.

COLEDALE INN,
Geoff Mawdsley,
Coledale Inn,
Braithwaite, Keswick,
CA12 5TN
T/F: 017687 78272/78416
E: info@coledale-inn.co.uk
W: www.coledale-inn.co.uk
R: 1S, 6D, 1T, 1F (bunks), 3D/F
B&B: £27-£32 EM: £6.95-£9.95. PL: £3.50

3 diamond. Home-made meals served for lunch and dinner in bar and
restaurant. Extensive range plus daily specials. Real ales, real country inn
sitting above the village. Comfortable and welcoming. Views of Skiddaw and
garden.

Cycle Repairs in Braithwaite. Ian Hindmarch fixes bikes in his
workshop next to the village stores , adjacent to the hump-back bridge
017687 78273.

KESWICK

Sandwiched between Derwentwater, Blencathra and Skiddaw at the entrance to the mighty Borrowdale valley, this market town is blessed with one of Britain's most idyllic settings. Ideal for cycling, walking, boating or just sightseeing, it is a favourite venue with cycle back-up teams; it is the most popular and best-equipped stop-off point on the route.

Keswick ('Cese-Wic' – the Cheese Town, literally) became prosperous in the 17th century during the reign of Elizabeth I, thanks to the mining of copper, lead, silver and iron. In order to run the mines engineers had to be imported from Germany. Despite a rocky start – local xenophobia drove them to inhabit Derwent Island – they soon managed to integrate. Evidence of this can be found in the phone book today, in the form of the many Germanic surnames.

The town's famous Cumberland Pencil Company came about after the discovery of graphite in Borrowdale in the 16th century. However, the town was granted its charter some 300 years before that by Edward I in 1276. Visitors started to flock in during the 18th century and in Victorian times many of them were literary pilgrims, attracted by the association with such Romantic poets as Southey, Coleridge and Wordsworth. John Ruskin, the aesthete and champion of the Pre-Raphaelites, had close associations with the town.

The population of the place has grown little in the past century. In 1902 there were 4,500 people; now there are just 500 more, but many of them – as you will note if you choose to stop over – are B&B owners. The place also has many good pubs and solid restaurants.

PLACES OF INTEREST

The Cumberland Pencil Museum, Near town centre 017687 73626
Cars of the Stars, Famous cars including a James Bondmobile, the Batmobile and Chitty Chitty Bang Bang 017687 73757
The Keswick Launch Company, tours on the lake, on the shore of Derwentwater 017687 72263.
George Fisher, big stock of outdoor gear, books and maps. Borrowdale Rd 017687 72178

Cotswold Outdoor Ltd, as above 017687 81939
The Moot Hall, Tourist Information Centre 017687 72645
Theatre by the Lake, Lakeside. Open all year round. Restaurant.
Beautiful setting. 017687 74411
Alhambra Cinema, St.Johns St 017687 72195
Castlerigg Stone Circle, thought to date from 3000 B.C. Steep climb
out of town on the alternative Penrith Rd route. Worth detour.
Keswick Museum & Art Gallery, interesting and eclectic collection
017687 72263

CYCLE SHOPS/ REPAIRS

Chris Warren, Kinniside, Portinscale 01768 72415
Keswick Mountain Bike Centre, Unit 1,Daleston Ct Daleston Court,
Southey Hill Industrial Estate, Keswick. 017687 75202
Keswick Riding and Cycle Hire Centre, cycle hire plus minor spares
and repairs.

WHERE TO EAT

Lemon & Lime, 31 Lake Road, international cuisine with tapas, pizzas
and other family favourites: 017687 73088
Salsa Mexican Bistro, 1 New Street, spicey and popular medium
priced establishment owned by the Nellist brothers: 017687 75222
Red Fort Indian Restaurant, 5 St John Street, lively and reliable spot
very popular with the locals: 017687 74328
Swinside Inn, Newlands, Keswick 017687 78253
Luca's Ristorante, High Hill, Greta Bridge, family run Italian with
elaborate decorations and prices to match: 017687 74621
Maysons Restaurant and Cafe, 33, Lake Road, Keswick, simple and
unpretentious eaterie. Good value: 017687 74104
The Bank Tavern, 47 Main St, solid, handsome pub with good,
traditional English cooking. Mediu price. Outside eating area: 017687
72663.
George Hotel, 3 St John St, medium priced fare: 017687 75751

THE MOUNT, Mr. & Mrs Ferguson,
Portinscale, Keswick, Cumbria CA12 5RD
T: 017687 73970

E: mount.ferguson@virgin.net

W: www.mountferguson.co.uk

R: 1S, 1D, 1T, 1F. B&B: £27 EM: no. PL: £6
Pub 200m, just 50m from route.
Locally independently inspected. Friendly,

family run and comfortable B&B in quiet setting. En-suite rooms. Splendid
lake/fell views. Excellent breakfasts with vegetarian options.

IVY LODGE, Barbara & Joseph Delin,
32 Penrith Road, Keswick, Cumbria CA12 4HA
T: 017687 75747

E: info@ivy-lodge.com W: www.ivylodge.com

R: 1D, 1T, 2F. B&B: £25. EM: no. PL: £4 Pub 5 minutes walk.
Good friendly house with good food, clean, with good parking.

ASH TREE HOUSE, Mrs Janet Redfearn,
Penrith Road, Keswick, Cumbria CA12 4LJ
T: 017687 72203

E: Peterredfearn@AOL.comW: www.ashtreehouse.co.uk

R: 1D, 1T. B&B: £20 - £27.
Pub 5 minutes walk. Newly built en-suites in each room, plenty of good off
road parking for support vehicles – see our web site.

HONISTER HOUSE, Sue Harrison,
1Borrowdale Road, Keswick, Cumbria, CA12 3DD
T: 017687 73181

E: philandsueh@aol.com

W: www.honisterhouse.co.uk

R: 1D, 1T, 1F. B&B: £26 - £35. EM: no. PL: £4
Pub 1 minute. 4 diamonds + Warm Welcome and

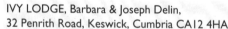

Sparkling Diamond awards. "We aim to exceed your expectations. A warm
welcome awaits you at our 18th-c home. Cyclists, walkers & families welcome.
Vegetarian option. Brochure available."

LAUREL BANK, P.R.& M.A. Roper,
Penrith Road, Keswick, Cumbria CA12 4LJ
T: 017687 73006 Mob: 07980 000 047
E: into@laurelbankkeswick.co.uk
W: www.laurelbankkeswick.co.uk
R: 2D, 1T, 2F (E-S). B&B £25 - £30. PL: £3.50-£4.50.
Pub 300m. Situated within 10 minutes walk of the
town centre, offering real breakfasts and Cumbrian

hospitality. Private car park and secure cycle storage.
All rooms are en-suite with fell views towards Grisedale Pike and Latrigg.

BECKSIDE, Mike & Gill Robertson,
5 Wordsworth St, Keswick CA12 4HU
T/F: 017687 73093
E: info@beckside-keswick.co.uk
W: www.beckside-keswick.co.uk
R: 2D, 1F, 2T. B&B: £25.
PL: £4. DFR: 300m.
ETB 3 Diamonds. This is a relaxed family
establishment. The breakfast has been described by
grateful cyclists as the 'best in the world,' comprising

just about everything and then some more; don't expect a fast getaway.
Rooms are en-suite, secure storage.

LINNETT HILL HOTEL,
Charles & Lorraine Carr,
4 Penrith Road, Keswick, CA12 4HF.
T/F: 017687 73109
E: info@linnetthillhotel.com
W: www.linnetthillhotel.com
R: 5D, 4T, 1S. B&B: from £27.
EM: no. PL: £5.
Pubs: surrounded by them.

Built in 1812, Linnett Hill has a Dutch façade and is charmingly situated with
views over Skiddaw and Latrigg. All rooms are en-suite. A family run hotel,
a personal service awaits you. Big private car park - room for 12 cars.

HALL GARTH, Keith & Tracy Baker,
37 Blencathra Street, Keswick, Cumbria CA12 4HX
T: 017687 72627
E: tracyhallgarth@aol.com
W: www.hall-garth.com
R: 4D/T, 2T. B&B: £22.50 - £25.
PL: £3.50. Pub 5 minutes. 4 Diamonds. Friendly, family run guest house.
Enjoy a full hearty English breakfast in our cosy dining room to set you on
your way.

GRASSMOOR GUEST HOUSE, Mike Hirst & Maureen Shirwell
10 Blencathra Street, Keswick, CA12 4HP.
T: 017687 74008
E: info@grassmoor-keswick.co.uk
W: www.grassmoor-keswick.co.uk
R: 4D, 4T, 2F, 2Tpl. B&B: £22.50 to £26.
EM: pubs and restaurants nearby. PL: £3.50
Pub 100m. 4 Diamonds. After a long day in the saddle settle down and relax
with a complimentary cuppas in a comfortable en-suite room at Mike and
Maureen's Cycle Friendly Guest House. We offer a variety of substantial
breakfasts to suit most appetites, cycle wash, laundry, baggage collection
and cycle recovery. Pubs and restaurants nearby.

TWA DOGS INN,
Peter & Marjorie Harding & family,
Penrith Rd, Keswick, CA12 4JU
T: 017687 72599
W: www.twadogs.co.uk
R: 1T, 1F (3S & 1D), 3D. (E-S).
B&B: £25pp.
Kids negotiable.

EM: <£5.95. PL: £4. SP: but not in restaurant.
Traditional family run Lakeland inn with an atmosphere as warm as the
welcome. Open fires, dominoes, darts & pool in a proper pub. Lock-up for
bikes and a range of real ales plus home-cooked food.

FERNDENE GUEST HOUSE,
Paul Bamber & Denise England,
6 St. John's Terrace, Ambleside Road,
Keswick, CA12 4DP. T: 017687 74612
E: ferndenekeswick@aol.com
W: www.ferndene-keswick.co.uk
R: 4D, 2T, 3F. B&B: £23-£26. EM: £5.50-£12 (3
courses). PL: £4.50. SP. Pub round corner. Full
Cumbrian breakfast with lots of choice. Vegetarian
options. Warm, cycle-friendly atmosphere. Open fires
in lounges, pool table, car park and outside garden
tables.

CHARNWOOD GUEST HOUSE,
Sue Banister,
6 Eskin Street,
Keswick CA12 4DH
T: 017687 74111
R: 3D, 2T, 1F.
B&B: £23-£35.
EM: available. PL: <£3.50.
4 diamonds.
Ornate Victorian 1850 listed building with elegant décor and excellent food.
All internal features original. Short level walk into the centre of Keswick.

DENTON HOUSE, Rebecca Chaffer,
Penrith Rd, Keswick, CA12 4JW
T: 017687 75351
E: sales@vividevents.co.uk
W: www.vividevents.co.uk
R: 8 containing 56 bunk beds.
B&B: £12. Breakfast for groups of 10 or more: £2.50
EM: groups of 20 or more: £5 - £7.50. PL: £5
Pub or restaurant: 100m. Budget accommodation run by Rebecca's bright
new company, Vivid Events. This is a big, friendly outdoor hostel, full of
youngsters. Lots of fun and cheerful.

Looking south down Derwent Water from Keswick **49**

Castlerigg Stone Circle above Keswick

There are two ways out of town. The most popular – and far the easier – is the one which follows the old Keswick-Penrith railway line and the river Greta as far as Threlkeld. It is a beautiful and leafy stretch. You get to it down Station Rd and Brundholme Rd, bearing left at the swimming pool and heading in front of the old station. Both routes assume the same start, unless you want to go out of Keswick along the old Penrith road.

A) The hard one. If you're feeling energetic and are (seriously) fit, then you'll prefer the Old Coach Road. It branches off the railway route on the edge of town, just before the track goes under the A66 viaduct. It then heads seriously steeply up to the 3,000 year old Castlerigg Stone Circle.

At this point you can come down and rejoin the more sedate option via Threlkeld and Mungrisdale, or you can press on through St John's in the Vale, Matterdale End and down to Greystoke via Hutton John. The Coach Road (what coach could possibly have tackled this?) is a seriously rough off-road alternative that is very exposed.

Check the weather before tackling it and don't do it if you're not certain of your capabilities. There is accommodation where the route crosses the A5091 at Matterdale (*see MATTERDALE P.55, TROUTBECK, and further along, just off the A66, PENRUDDOCK & MOTHERBY*) before the route rejoins the easier alternative at GREYSTOKE (see p. 57). **B) The not so hard one.** This takes you fairly effortlessly the five kilometres or so to Threlkeld, though you can make it slightly tougher by taking in the Castlerigg Stone Circle detour at the start of the alternative (*see above*) before heading back onto the easy lower road.

THRELKELD

Blencathra, known locally as Saddleback, overlooks this traditional and pretty Cumbrian village. There are also views towards Clough Head and the Helvellyn range. Threlkeld is, I gather, Norse for 'the spring of the thrall' – thrall being a bonded servant. Zinc, lead and granite were mined during the last century until the last of the granite miners hung up their shovels and picks in the mid-80s. At one time more than a hundred men were employed. At the quarry there is a mining museum with an impressive mineral collection, mining artefacts and touching reminders of how things used to be. A table top relief map of the Lake District and a pictorial history of Threlkeld are also on display. There was once a TB isolation hospital which is now a field centre for biologists and geographers. Since the Dark Ages and the days of Sir Lancelot de Threlkeld, hunting has been an integral part of local life; this is the home of the Blencathra Hunt, the famous Lakeland pack that hunts on foot rather than horseback. The famous Threlkeld sheepdog trials feature foxhound and terrier shows, and hound trailing. All of which, one presumes, has come to a sad end this year.

HORSE & FARRIER INN, Lee Barrett,
Threlkeld,
nr Keswick
CA12 4SQ.
T: 017687 79688
F: 017687 79824
E: info@horseandfarrier.com
W: www.horseandfarrier.com
R: 2S, 6D, 1T (SP: designated areas)
B&B: £35.
EM: £5.95 - £15.
PL: £5.
On route. Lock-up/drying facilities

4 Diamonds, AA & RAC approved: A beautifully restored 17th century inn offering award winning food and drink with comfortable accommodation. Idyllic location in centre of village, it sits at the foot of Blencathra. Serves great real ales and food. Comfortable, en-suite rooms.
Listed in AA Pub, AA Restaurant and AA Hotel guides.

THE HOLLIES,
John & Margaret Fleet,
Threlkeld,
nr Keswick
CA12 4RX
T: 017687 79216
M: 07887 611127
E: info@theholliesinlakeland.co.uk
W: www.theholliesinlakeland.co.uk
R: 4T/D. B&B: £27.
EM: no - pubs and food nearby.
PL: £3.50

AA 4 diamonds.
Fine stone-built house with spectacular views to front and rear.
John & Margaret have been in the hotel business for 30 years so know how to look after you.
Ample parking. Great breakfast.

Skiddaw and Blencathra dominate the whole valley

SCALES

After Threlkeld there is a short section along a car-free country road, then a cycle path alongside the A66 until Scales, where you go along a delightful gated lane into Mungrisdale. Look up from the road and admire Blencathra on your left and the Helvellyn range to the right.

SCALES FRAM COUNTRY GUEST HOUSE,
Alan & Angela Jameison,
Scales, Threlkeld,
Nr Keswick, CA12 4SY
T: 017687 79660 F: 017687 79510
E: scales@scalesfarm.com
W: www.scalesfarm.com

R: 3D, 1F, 2T/D (E-S). B&B: £29-£32.
EM: pub next door, or other nearby hostelries. PL: £4.50.
ETB 4-diamonds. Modernised 17th century Lakeland farmhouse at the foot of Blencathra overlooking the northern Lake District fells. Trad & vegetarian breakfasts. Immaculate throughout.

MUNGRISDALE

This delightful village was added to the route in 2001 and a welcome addition it is. It comprises a traditional inn, a church and a cluster of houses all huddled around the bubbling river Glenderamackin. A truly restful spot, as you reach it along the gated road you have spectacular views of the fells; Souther and Blencathra (better known in these parts as Saddleback) to the West, and the Ullswater fells to the South. And to the east, the daunting prospect of the Pennines. St Kentigern church is mid-18th century and the Mill Inn is even older.

Its position on the river makes it a natural stopping-off point, an excellent place to stretch the legs and take photographs. The valley is hemmed in by the lowering Cumbrian range but on a good day it is a

THE MILL INN, Jim & Margaret Hodge,
Mungrisdale, nr Penrith, Cumbria CA11 0XR
T: 017687 79632
F: 017687 79981
E: margaret@the-millinn.co.uk
W: www.the-millinn.co.uk

R: 3D, 3T. B&B: £35.
EM: £4-£20. PL: <£4. SP: bar.
3 diamonds. Traditional 17th inn. Beautiful location. Log fire, warm welcome, excellent accommodation. Home-made food and cask ales.

veritable sun trap - and a tempting proposition for an overnight stay.

The Sustrans route suggests you cross the river just a few hundred metres short of the village, but that would be a shame. If you go as far as the pub you can take the alternative path out of Mungrisdale over minor lanes and through Berrier and onto the Greystoke road, or simply follow the lane back down the other side of the Glendermackin to the A66, where a cycle path takes over.

At the top of the hill you can follow the route to the left or carry straight on for Greystoke. Either will do; the former will take you to Penruddock and neighbouring Motherby, where there is excellent accommodation just 4km south of Greystoke.

Blencow Hall, one of several fortified farmhouses in the area

MATTERDALE

Greenah B&B (below) is at the Thatckthwaite end of the old Coach Road, so is close to the A66 and handy for those tackling both the normal route and the cross-country alternative. Marjorie Emery is a keen Sustrans supporter and is doing her bit for the C2C.

GREENAH, Marjorie Emery,
Matterdale End,
nr Penrith, CA11 0SA
T&F: 01768 483387
E: greenah@tiscali.co.uk
W: www.greenah.co.uk
R: 2D. B&B: £27-£34.
EM: no – lift provided to local pub.
PL: £5. Newly inspected.

Friendly, comfortable accommodation in a quiet location with superb views, nestling under Little Mell Fell and close to Ullswater. Local and home-made produce, private bathroom facilities.

PENRUDDOCK

THE HERDWICK INN,
Lee Barrett & Ian Court,
Penruddock, Nr Penrith,
CA11 0QU
T: 017684 83007 F: 017684 80391
E: info@herdwickinn.com
W: www.herdwickinn.com
R: 1T, 3D, 1S (E-S). B&B: £35.

ETB 4-diamonds, AA & RAC approved.
EM: from £7.50 to £17. PL: <£3.50. SP: bar.
On B5288 to Greystoke – alternative route through Motherby.
18th century village inn with oak beams and stonework, woodburning
stove, range of real ales and mezzanine restaurant serving traditional English
fare made from local ingredients by a local chef. The emphasis here is on
food and drink with comfortable accommodation.

MOTHERBY

MOTHERBY HOUSE,
Mrs Jacquie Freeborn,
Motherby,
nr Penrith,
Cumbria CA11 0RJ
T: 017684 83368
E: jacquie@enterprise.net
W: www.motherbyhouse.co.uk
R: 2F.
B&B: £20.
EM:£13.50 (by prior notice).

PL: £5. SP: designated areas.
Pub 1.5km.
On B5288.
Warm friendly former 18th century farmhouse.
Excellent food for outdoor appetites and muddy boots welcome.

View from St John's churchyard, Keswick

GREYSTOKE

This traditional English village, 8km west of Penrith, was built around a green with a pretty pub and a church the size of a cathedral. Discretely hidden at the top of a long drive and behind a curtain of trees in a 3,000 acre wooded park is Greystoke Castle, seat of the Howard family for the last five centuries.

Tarzan is modelled on one former Baron Greystoke of this parish, and there are certainly enough trees for any Lord of the Apes to practise on. Not much is made of the Tarzan connection on the estate, but that is because it is a family home and business rather than a tourist theme park. However, I thought Tarzan fans might be interested to know.

The origins of Greystoke are probably Roman – they built a road from Penrith to Troutbeck. The name itself means 'place by the River

Creik', a small stream nearby. Indeed, the village was known as Creistock in early Medieval times.

Though most of the village dates from the 17th century, the foundation of the Perpendicular-style church was laid in mid-1200s, but building did not start until 1382 and went on into the next century. The bells that still ring out in Greystoke date from the Middle Ages. Inside the church is some fine Medieval and Victorian stained glass. It is simply a magnificent church, a splendid monument to the wealth of the great Howard family.

The Spillers Stone in the village was thought to be a plague stone, where plague victims left coins in a pool of vinegar on its concave surface. The vinegar was added to protect the healthy, who left food there for sufferers.

According to the Cumbria Directory, Greystoke Castle, the seat of the Howard family from the 1500's, was an integral part of village life. The first stone building to occupy the site was constructed in 1129 and served as protection against raids from Scottish Border raiders, or

Reivers, as they were known in the days before the famous cycle route assumed the nomenclature.

Cromwell destroyed much of Greystoke and a devastating fire in 1868 ensured that only the medieval pele (fortified) tower and a few Georgian interiors survived. The present building, in the Elizabethan style, dates from the 19th century.

The nearby countryside boasts a number of fine old fortified houses complete with pele towers, notably Blencow Hall, built in 1590, Greenthwaite Hall, and Johnby Hall. All are reminders of the bloody times of the Border Reivers.

The Boot and Shoe Pub was acquired its name because of the strange sartorial habit of a former Duke of Norfolk of wearing a shoe on one foot and a boot on the other, to ease the pain of crippling gout. Whether or not, thus clad, he shuffled down the long drive and across the green to the pub is not recorded.

BRATHEN, Christine Mole,
The Thorpe, Greystoke,
nr Penrith, Cumbria CA11 0TJ
T/F: 017684 83595
E: stay@brathen.co.uk
W: www.brathen.co.uk
R: 2D, 2T, 1F. B&B: £22.50. PL:£4. SP. DFR: 300m. Pub 300m.
Comfortable barn conversion on the outskirts of the village with a warm welcome and hearty breakfasts using local produce.

BOOT & SHOE INN,
Paul Cobbe, Greystoke,
Nr Penrith, CA11 0TP
T: 017684 83343
E: paul@bootshoe.fsbusiness.co.uk
R: 2D, 2T. B&B: <£22.50. SP: bar only.
16th century coaching inn, open fires, local ales and home-made food. Next door to

Greystoke Castle of Tarzan fame, it is a lively village pub serving robust food and good ale and has newly refurbished bedrooms.

MELDENE, Mrs Ann Cooper,
Icold Road, Greystoke,
nr Penrith, Cumbria CA11 0UG
T: 017684 83856
R: 1D, 1T. B&B: £20. PL: £4.
Pub 300m. Small friendly B&B near village centre. Locally inspected. Aga
breakfast, clothes drying, secure garage for cycles.

LATTENDALES FARM, Mrs Jean Ashburner,
Berrier Road, Greystoke,
nr Penrith CA11 0UE
T: 017684 83474
R: 2D + 1T. B&B: £19-£20. PL.
Pub 400yds. Locally inspected. 17th century farmhouse of character with
comfortable accommodation, well recommended by cyclists.

The route out of Greystoke goes past Blencow Hall, the
aforementioned fortified farmhouse. It is an unusually handsome
building just before you get to the village of Little Blencow. Just up the
road follow signs to the right and you will enter Penrith via Newton
Reigny and Newton Rigg.

NEWTON REIGNY

THE SUN INN, Dennis Dixon,
Newton Reigny,
Nr Penrith, CA11 0AP
T: 01768 867055
E: dixond@tinyworld.co.uk
W: www.uktouristinfo.co.uk
R: 1T, 2F, 2D (E-S).

B&B: £30 pp, £75 fam. EM: £6.50 - £14.50. PL: £5.
17th century inn bordering the River Petteril. Nice bar and some fine real
ales. There's a 60-seater restaurant and a lovely beer garden. Secure lock-
up for bikes. Closed 3-6pm weekdays.

NEWTON RIGG

CUMBRIAN CAMPUS AT NEWTON RIGG,
Janet Rowbury,
Newton Rigg,
Penrith,
Cumbria CA11 0AH
T: 01768 863791 F: 01768 844998
E: cumbriainfo@uclan.ac.uk
W: www.conferencecumbria.co.uk
R: 270S, 18T. B&B: £20-£23.
EM: £8.95 (3-courses). PL: £3.90
Pub on site. Standard & en-suite rooms. Meals available to non-residents.
Secure cycle sheds. Shops. Laundrette.

PENRITH

On leaving Newton Rigg campus go underneath the M6 and turn
right at the T-junction, going into town along Robinson Street, across
Scotland Rd and into Drover's Lane. The route is well sign-posted.
You know you are on the right tracks when you find yourself exiting
Penrith up Fell Lane – a steep climb to a T-junction at the top, where I
once saw a cyclist being overtaken by a pedestrian carrying shopping.

The town itself is a handsome red sandstone market borough,
and was the capital of the Kingdom of Cumbria in the 9th and 10th
centuries, at a time when the area was allied to Scotland. Semi-
independent, it was also part of the Kingdom of 'Scotland Strathclyde'
and was historically always on the main north-south road between
England and Scotland. Much bloody action was witnessed during the
border conflicts; indeed the Scots, envious of its prosperity, torched the
town three times during the 14th century.

Until the end of the 14th century Penrith had no water supply. But
in 1385 Bishop Strickland diverted Thacka Beck from the river Peterill,
and an eco-sensitive agreement allowed the townspeople to draw daily
only as much water from the Peterill as would flow through the eye of
a millstone. You can see the millstone outside the Tourist Information
Centre.

William & Dorothy Wordsworth's school - where the poet met his wife

By the 18th century it was an important cattle market and the oldest streets in the town Burrowgate and Sandgate – are narrow, unspoilt and 800 years old. The Gloucester Arms pub is thought to date from 1477 and is supposed to have been Richard III's favourite hostelry. The Two Lions is equally historic, while the George Hotel provided lodgings for Bonnie Prince Charlie in 1745, when on his ill-fated foray south to claim the crown.

Other famous names associated with the town include Mary Queen of Scots, Oliver Cromwell and the writer, Anthony Trollope. The former must have spent most of her life on horseback in order to get to the places she is alleged to have visited and stayed at, though in the case of Penrith, the connection is entirely justified. Oliver Cromwell, meanwhile, occupied the town in 1654. Whilst the pen may be mightier than the sword, Trollope is not thought to have caused much bloodshed here.

Two old-fashioned shops have survived, as if preserved in aspic:

Graham's, Penrith's answer to Fortnum & Mason; and Arnisons, the drapers, established in 1740 and once the home of Wordsworth's grandparents. The poet and his sister Dorothy attended the Dame Anne Birkett School, now the Tudor Coffee Room, overlooking St Andrew's Churchyard and final resting place of a legendary giant and King of All Cumbria.

Penrith Castle, a splendidly ruined sandstone edifice in the public park, dates from the 14th century, built onto an existing pele tower. In 1471 it became a royal fortress for the Duke of Gloucester (later Richard III) who was 'Guardian of the West March towards Scotland.'

Legend has it that a passageway existed to the Gloucester Arms, for His Majesty's safe passage to a tap room. Much of the stonework from the castle – by the mid-1500s, a ruin – has become incorporated in the town's buildings, just as much of the fabric of Hadrian's Wall has metamorphosed into smallholdings, churches and houses in much of the surrounding countryside.

Above Penrith is Beacon Hill, past which you will shortly be cycling. Beacons have been lit there through the ages to warn of threat of invasion. It offers some of the most stunning views across the Eden Valley to the Pennines.

In more recent times the area was immortalised in Bruce Robinson's classic film comedy of 1987, 'Withnail and I', in which the area is once again traumatised - this time by a pair of drunken wannabe actors from London.

PLACES OF INTEREST

The Penrith Museum & Tourist Information Centre are housed in the former Robinson's School, an Elizabethan building which was altered in 1670 and used as a school until the early 1970's. The recently refurbished museum covers the history, geology and archaeology of the Penrith area. Free. 01768 867466

St Andrew's Church: The Giant's Grave in the Churchyard: was it Tarquin, the slayer of women, or Owen Caesarius, King of Cumbria? Grave thought to be 10th century.

Bluebell Bookshop, Angel Sq. Old-fashioned place with good travel section and mapping: **01768 866660.**

Architecture – take a walk around. Well worth a stopover. There are several market areas all linked by wonderful narrow streets. You can see how security was in the mind of early planners.

EATING OUT

Bewicks Coffee Shop & Bistro, Princes Court, accomplished and simple; lovely setting, reasonable prices: 01768 864764
Taste of Bengal, Stricklandgate, solid and unpretentious dishes from a place without pretentions: 01768 891700
George Hotel, Devonshire St, does everything from lounge snacks to formal restaurant. Reliable and reasonable: 01768 862696
Peaberrys Restaurant & Cafe, Angel Sq, smart in-and-out eaterie, reasonable prices: 01768 890170
Platinum Chinese Restaurant, buffet more than adequate - some rave reports from other diners: 01768 210210.
Blue Elephant Café, Angel Sq, vegetarian organic retreat upstairs from the Bluebell Bookshop. New cafe owner: 01768 866660.
Scotts Fish Restaurant, Sandgate, 53-seat no-nonsense chippie next to the bus station: 01768 890838.

CYCLE SHOPS

Arragons, Brunswick Road 01768 890 344

Harpers Cycles, 1-2 Middlegate 01768 864 475

HELTON, PENRITH

Helton is 10km from Penrith, in the fells near Ullswater. You can either hack your way across from Hutton John, near where the Coach Road joins the A6 by Penruddock, or you can take the B5320 out of Eamont Bridge, turning left at Yanwath onto the Askham road. It's 5km down there.

BECKFOOT COUNTRY HOUSE,
David & Lesley White, Helton,
Nr. Penrith,
Cumbria, CA10 2QB
T: 01931 713 241
F: 01931 713 391
E: info@beckfoot.co.uk
W: www.beckfoot.co.uk
R: 1S, 3D, 1T, 1F, 1 four poster.
B&B £35 - £48 .
EM: snacks available. PL: £4.50.
DFR: 10km. Pub 3km

4 diamonds. Small family run bed and breakfast run by the Whites for the past 27 years. Ideal for walking, biking and geting away from it all. Popular with C2Cers, despite distance from route. Your hosts are perfectly happy to ferry you to and from pubs and eateries.

PENRITH CENTRE

NORCROFT GUEST HOUSE,
Tim & Elizabeth Blagbrough,
Graham Street,
Penrith,
Cumbria
CA11 9LQ
T: 01768 862 365
F: 01768 210 425
E: info@norcroft-guesthouse.co.uk
W: www.norcroft-guesthouse.co.uk
R: 1S, 1D, 4T/D, 2F, 1Tpl.
B&B: £23.50-£30.
EM: £12-£15.
PL: £4.
Pub 200m. 4 diamonds.

Family run, licensed guest house. The Norcroft is a large Victorian house, accommodating up to 22 guests. Secure covered storage for bikes.

BRANDELHOW GUEST HOUSE,
Lanie & Mel Hancox,
1 Portland Place,
Penrith,
Cumbria, CA11 7QN
T: 01768 864470

W: www.brandelhowguesthouse.co.uk
E: enquiries@brandelhowguesthouse.co.uk
R: 1S, 2D/T, 1T, 2F (one of which sleeps six people).
B&B: £26. PL: £5 Pub 50m.
3 diamonds. Victorian town house, close to the town centre, ideally
situated for the C2C cycle route and walking holidays in the Lakes.

GLENDALE GUEST HOUSE,
Nancy Phillips & Moira Barrett,
4 Portland Place, Penrith, Cumbria, CA11 7QN
T: 01768 862579

E: glendaleguesthouse@yahoo.co.uk
W: www.glendaleguesthouse.com
R: 1S, 2D, 2T, 2F. B&B: £25-£36. PL: £4.
Restaurant & pub:100m. 4 diamonds. "Spacious rooms
in a Victorian town house with friendly, comfortable
atmosphere. Ideal stopover where, after a good night's rest, the famous
Glendale hearty breakfast will set you up for the climb to Alston and
beyond!"

EDEN GATE, Lorraine Roberts,
5 Victoria Road, Penrith,
CA11 8HR
T: 01768 866538
E: edengate@edengate.net
W: www.edengate.net
R: 1D, 1T, 2F. B&B £22.50 - £28
Pub 100m. Friendly, homely atmosphere with comfortable rooms, delicious
breakfast, secure cycle parking and location within two to three minutes
walk of Penrith's shops and restaurants.

ALBANY HOUSE, Mr & Mrs Bell,
5 Portland Place, Penrith CA11 7QN.
T/F: 01768 863072
E: info@albany-house.org.uk
W: www. albany-house.org.uk
R: 2D, 2F, 1T/Tpl. B&B £22-£27.50 PL: £4
Pub 50m. 3 diamond/Sparkling Diamond/Warm
Welcome Award.
Lovely mid-Victorian town house close to town
centre. Hospitality tray. Drying facilities, secure
bike storage. Hearty breakfasts and the warmest of
welcomes.

CALEDONIA GUEST HOUSE,
Ian & Sue Rhind, 8 Victoria Road,
Penrith, CA11 8HR
T: 01768864482
E: i.Rhind@virgin.net
W: www.caledoniaguesthouse.co.uk
R: 2D, 2T, 1F. B&B: £25-£30. PL: £5. DFR:
700m. Pub 200m. Victorian town house close to town centre. Comfortable
rooms with TV, tea & coffee making facilities. Excellent breakfast!.

ROUNDTHORN COUNTRY HOUSE,
Meini Canniffe,
Beacon Edge, Penrith,
Cumbria, CA11 8JS
T: 01768 863952 F: 01768 864100
E: enquiries@roundthorn.co.uk
W: www.roundthorn.co.uk
R: 8D, 1T, 2F (E-S). B&B: £37.50-£61
EM: £7.50-£9.50. PL: £4.50. (licensed)
Pub 1km. 5 Diamond Award.

A beautiful Georgian mansion with spectacular views of the Eden Valley
& Lakeland Fells. All rooms are en-suite with TV and tea/coffee making
facilties. The hotel has a licensed bar.

LANGWATHBY

Go to the top of Fell Lane and turn right onto Beacon Edge. There are fabulous views from here followed by a long descent to the B6412. Enjoy it while you can; the really serious bit is about to start.

Soon you are at Langwathby, a village built around a large green, on the banks of the river Eden. There's a pub, shop and even a railway station which services the popular Carlisle to Settle line. This area – which includes the charming villages of **Edenhall, Little Salkeld** and **Great Salkeld** – are popular overnight stops because they are strategically well-placed for attacking Hartside and the other hills that make the next section the hardest. Melmerby, on the A686 about 5km from Langwathby is also popular. There's a pub there, a famous bakery and limited B&B.

Langwathby was a Viking settlement; Edenhall once boasted a fine stately home and Little Salkeld, with its watermill, is about 3km away – close to Long Meg and Little Meg stone circles. Long Meg comprises a megalith at the head of 60 stones some 360ft (115m) in diameter.

EDEN HALL COUNTRY HOTEL
& RESTAURANT,
Clare & Tony Simmons,
Edenhall,
Langwathby,
Cumbria
CA11 8SX.
T: 01768 881454
F: 01768 881266
E: info@edenhallhotel.co.uk
W: www.edenhallhotel.co.uk

R: 5S, 9D, 7T (E-S).
B&B: <£35. EM: £6.45-£17 (3-courses)
Hotel has public bar. 2 Star country house hotel in beautiful surroundings. Sky TV, telephone, tea/coffee in all rooms. Great chef. Secure cycle storage and drying facilities. Telephone for brochure. Emphasis on quality food has resulted in one AA Rosette.

LANGSTANES, Clive Gravett,
Culgaith Road, Langwathby, nr Penrith CA10 1NA
T: 01768 881 004
E: samclive@langstanes.wanadoo.co.uk
W: www.langstanes.co.uk
R: 2D, 1T (E-S). B&B: £24.50. PL: £3.50
Pub 200m. Local inspection: commended. Comfortable sandstone house on route, tea/coffee-making facilities, colour TV, secure bike storage, drying facilities.

LITTLE SALKELD
BANK HOUSE FARM,
Raymond Atkinson,
Little Salkeld,
Penrith, Cumbria CA10 1NN
T: 01768 881 257
E: bankhouseequ@aol.com
R: 4D, 2T, 2F. B&B: from £25.
PL: £4.50. SP. Pub 2km. B&B, self -catering, camping in converted cottages for individuals, families or larger groups. Secure cycle storage. A warm friendly family welcome awaits.

GREAT SALKELD
Left down the B6412 where you turn right for Langwathby – it's 3km.

THE HIGHLAND DROVE INN
& KYLOES RESTAURANT, Donald Newton,
Great Salkeld, Penrith, Cumbria CA11 9NA
T: 01768 898349. F: 01768 898708
E: highlanddroveinn@btinternet.com
W: www.highland-drove.co.uk
R: 3D, 2T. (SP in pub) B&B: £25-£30 PL: £5. EM:
Starters <£3.50 Mains <£7.95 Sweets <£2.50

DFR: 3km. A real country pub with open fires, real ale, quality wines and beer garden. Separate restaurant 'Le Routier'. Affiliated bistro with eclectic cuisine, Routier-rated. CAMRA Winter Pub of the Season. Routier Dining Pub of the North & CAMRA local Pub of the Year.

69

The handsome market town of Alston

ALSTON... AND INTO THE PENNINES

The hill out of Little Salkeld is very steep. Stop off and do some sightseeing, says my esteemed colleague and C2C expert, Dik Stoddart: "Visit Long Meg – it's an excuse to have a rest."

You will shortly be presented with an choice: whether or not to take the cross-country route over Hartside. If you do you will be pushing or carrying your bike for quite a bit of the stretch. If you take the alternative road route via Renwick you will have a winding and steep ascent, but one that is manageable from the saddle (I suspect that I'm not the only cyclist to have dismounted a couple of times on this section).

At the top is Hartside Café, a (motor)bikers haven. At 580 metres (1900 feet), it is the highest tea shop in England and on a fine day (they do happen) you can see Scotland across the Solway Firth. Views of the

Eden Valley are terrific: not for nothing was the drive along the A686 voted one of the ten best in the world by the AA Magazine.

Your climb up to Hartside is rewarded by one of the best sections of downhill in the North West. Near the bottom of Benty Hill a road goes off to the right for Leadgate and Garrigill. You have a choice – take it, or continue the delirious descent along the A686 until you get to the handsome town of Alston, perched on the edge of the Pennines.

The hamlet of Leadgate is on the Garrigill road – though you can get back on the Alston road by continuing out of the village instead of heading right.

Alston sits at 280m (919feet) above sea level and is supposedly the highest market town in England. Picture-postcard-pretty and a firm favourite with outdoor types, it lies in a designated Area of Outstanding Natural Beauty (AONB), a solid bastion of civilisation on the edge of one of Britain's greatest areas of wilderness.

A former centre for Cumberland wrestling, cattle fairs and races, Alston is completely unspoilt by developers and has cobbled streets, 17th century shops and pubs that hark back to a former age. It is naturally a magnet for film makers; Oliver Twist was shot here for television – there is even an Oliver Twist trail – and Dickens himself visited in the 1830s to research Nicholas Nickleby, one of his novels.

The town, built around an old market square, was formed around the confluence of the South Tyne and Nent rivers and owes much to the lead mining industry. First mined by the Romans, the Quakers arrived in the 18th century to set up the London Lead Mining Company.

To find out more, visit the Mines Heritage Centre. The mines and their machinery are now silent but there are scattered hill farms where mining families grew crops to subsidise their meagre wages. Heather clad moors, fells and valleys are alive with curlews, lapwings, peewits, peregrines and grouse, while deer and red squirrel roam this natural fastness.

There is some fine cycling across Alston Moor before you get to Nenthead. You can either take the B6277 past Garrigill or take the more direct A689.

PLACES OF INTEREST

Tourist Information Centre: Town Hall, Front St 01434 382244.

South Tynedale Railway Station – England's highest narrow-gauge track runs along 3.6km of former British Rail track. There is a tea room at the old station. Runs every weekend April – October plus some weekends in December, and daily during August. 01434 381696 or, for the talking timetable 01434 382828.

Hartside Nursery Garden - one mile from Alston: rare alpine plants

EATING OUT

Alston House *is a welcome addition (see entry)* 01434 382200

Blueberry's in the Market Place – good meals, snacks and afternoon tea. 01434 381928.

The Cumberland Hotel – *(see entry)* 01434 381875.

The Moody Baker – artisan bakery owned by a workers' co-operative specialising in delicious pies, quiches etc and originators of the high-energy Moody Baker Biker Bar 01434 382003.

Gossipgate Gallery – arts & crafts, coffee & cakes 01434 381806.

Alston's medieval market place

ALSTON HOUSE, Michael & Sarah Glass,
Townfoot, Alston, Cumbria CA9 3RN
T: 01434 382200
E: enquiries@alstonhouse.co.uk
W: www.alstonhouse.co.uk
R: 1D,1T, 3F, 1Tpl, 2D+S, 1D+2S.
B&B: from £28. EM: £7-£15. PL: £4. SP in bar.
Attractive and comfortable family run hotel. B&B

in an historic listed building. Strong emphasis on quality but affordable food.
Themed 1940s dinning room.

VICTORIA INN, Steve & Tian Smith,
Front Street, Alston,
Cumbria CA9 3SE
T/F: 01434 381194
E: victoriainncumbria@talk21.com
R: 4S, 2D, 2F (1D+1F E-S)
B&B: £16.50 to £22.50. SP. EM: <£2.95. PL: £3.50
Friendly family run town inn/B&B on the route.

Fine beers, bar & restaurant meals (Chinese & Indian speciality) C2C, bikers
and walkers welcome.

THE CUMBERLAND HOTEL,
Guy & Helen Harmer,
Town Foot, Alston, Cumbria CA9 3HX
T: 01434 381 875
E: helenguyh@aol.com
R: 2D, 1F, 2Tpl.
B&B: £26-£31.
EM: £5-£15.
PL: £4.
All rooms en-suite, bike storage, drying/cleaning facilities.Only stamping
point in Alston. Choice of traditional cask ales & home cooked food.
Family run.

YHA, The Firs, Alston, CA9 3RW
T: 0870 770 5668 F: 0870 770 5669
E: alston@yha.org.uk W: www.yha.org.uk
EM: £5.20. PL: £3.20-£4.10. Breakfast: £3.60. Bunkrooms: 2x2, 2x4, 3x6
30 bedded purpose built youth hostel, secure cycle storage, drying room,
catered or self-catering, 5 minutes walk from town centre.

GARRIGILL

Now a village of some 200 souls, it once had a thriving population of
1,000 thanks to the lead mining. It is a lovely, sleepy village, complete
with green, pub and post office. Some of the hardest riding is ahead, so
for many it makes a natural overnight stop-off, especially if you have
slogged all the way from the fells west of Penrith.

For those who like an extra challenge there is the tough route out of
the village, up the very steep and rough track onto the B6277, then left
onto a forest track and down into Nenthead the hard way.

GEORGE & DRAGON, Richard & Julia Jackson,
Garrigill, Alston, CA9 3DS
T: 01434 381293. F: 01434 382839
E: thegeorgeanddragon@btopenworld.com
R: 2S, 1T, 1D (E-S). B&B: £21-£22.
EM: £2.95-£8.95. PL: £4.50
Historic 17th century inn, overlooking a sunny village green, which offers
comfortable bedrooms, good home cooked food and three cask ales.

HIGH WINDY HALL HOTEL,
Mrs Pauline Platts,
Middleton in Teesdale Road,
(onB6277), Garrigill, CA9 3EZ
T: 01434 381547 F: 01434 382477
E: sales@hwh.u-net.com. W: www.hwh.u-net.com
R: 2D, 1T, 1F. B&B: £30. EM: £18-£23. PL: £4
DFR: 200 metres. Pub 2km. ETB 4 diamonds. Family-run licensed hotel,
good food, interesting wine list, peaceful views overlooking South Tyne
Valley, well-deserved luxury after Hartside Pass. All bedrooms en-suite.

NENTHEAD

Folk in both Nenthead and Allenheads – the next port of call
– claim to live in England's highest village. I would be interested to
know definitively which is the higher. Either way, Nenthead is 500m
above sea level and has a colder climate than Aberdeen. It does seem
incredible that only 300 million years ago it was on the equator.

The village was purpose-built for mining in 1825 by the Quaker
Lead Company. In addition to housing they provided a reading room,
wash-house, public baths and a school for the 1500 employees in the
Methodist stronghold. At weekends they ran smallholdings and this

THE MINERS ARMS, Alison Clark,
Nenthead, Alston,
Cumbria CA9 3PF
T: 01434 381427
E: minersarms@cybermoor.org.uk
W: www.nenthead.com
Bunkhouse: £11 (Sleeps 15) B'fast £4.
EM: £4.50-£7.50. PL: £3.50.
SP: but not in bunkhouse.
A rider writes: 'C2Cing again. Second

time, and the hospitality is just as good, if not better. Great food, friendly
welcome.'

MILL COTTAGE BUNK HOUSE, Ray Hall,
Nenthead, Alston, Cumbria CA9 3PD
T: 01434 382726
F: 01434 382294
E: administrationoffice@virgin.net
Beds: 12. Bed only £10.
Pub nearby. Superior quality bunkhouse accommodation. Right on C2C route. Set amidst spectacular scenery within heritage centre site. Washing/drying facilties. Fully fitted kitchen. Secure cycle storage.

CHERRY TREE COTTAGE, Hellen Sherlock,
Nenthead, Alston, Cumbria CA9 3PD
T: 01434 381434
R: 4D, 5F.
B&B £18-£22. EM: no. PL: £3.50
On route, Pub: 100m
Warm, comfortable accommodation set high up in the North Pennines. It is right on the route and there are TVs in all rooms. Pub and restaurant just on the doorstep. We especially welcome walkers and cyclists.

way of life lasted for more than 100 years. A decorative fountain in the middle of the village serves as a memorial to R.W.Bainbridge Esq, superintendent of the mine company.

Falling markets, however, destroyed the community; cheap imports lead to a collapse in prices, and many families emigrated to the USA and Australia at the end of the 19th century. Zinc mining continued until the 1940s and Nenthead Mines eventually closed its last pit in 1961.

PLACES OF INTEREST

The Nenthead Mines Heritage Centre is a must. They have brought to life the old workings on this 200 acre site and have helped breath life into a village that history somehow forgot. You can even do some mineral panning and visit the sites on self-guided trails.

Killhope Lead Mining Centre is off the A689 5km east of Nenthead. Underground visits possible April – October. 01388 537505.

BICYCLE REPAIRS

Mark Fearn – the village blacksmith also repairs bikes, stocks spares and will do a breakdown and recovery service if needed 01434 382194.

ALLENHEADS

This is a pretty unremitting stretch with the steepest climb coming directly out of Nenthead, so if you are staying overnight avoid one of those typically generous and massive Cumbrian breakfasts.

Turn left off the A689 after just over a kilometre of hellish gradient, past the disused lead mineshafts, and soon you will be crossing the highest point on the route – Black Hill. At 609 metres (just a tad under 2000 feet) it is 29 metres (nearly 100 feet) higher than Hartside. Once you have conquered the climb up past Killhope Law it's pretty plane sailing down to Allenheads.

This is a truly delightful village nestling amongst the trees. Its focal point is a marvellous little pub called the Allenheads Inn where a cornucopia of fascinating nick knacks are suspended from ceilings and walls, doors and passageways.

A century ago this prosperous and peaceful little haven was a toneless grey valley of slag heaps shrouded by smog, for it too was a mining community which provided one sixth of the nation's requirement for lead. The village slipped into decline when the bottom fell out of the industry but has done amazingly well in recent years to revitalise itself. There is now a Trust, a visitor centre plus mining exhibitions and a shop and café.

This is the home of the British Norwegian Ski Club. There are three tow ropes taking you to the top of the run at 540 metres. Annual family membership is £30, which covers towing, hire of the rope and passes; facilities on the piste also include a small bait hut where there is a BYO gluwein facility.

Apres ski is in the pub. An ideal place for celebrities, it is usually free of paparazzi and gossip columnists. A popular haunt with the beau monde of Carlisle and Newcastle, Allenheads is once again a coming place.

PLACES OF INTEREST

Heritage Centre – next to the babbling beck, you can't miss it.
Woodland Nature Trail – walks that take you around the village.
Old Blacksmith's Shop – smithy with display.
The Allenheads Trust, Allenheads Heritage Centre, T/F: 0l434 685043

THE ALLENHEADS INN,
Stephen & Sue Wardle, Allenheads,
Hexham, Northumberland NE47 9HJ
T/F: 0l434 685200
E: theallenheadsinn@yahoo.co.uk
W: www.theallenheadsinn.co.uk
R: 3D,2T,1S, 1F
B&B: £20-£27.50 (credit cards welcome).
EM: <£5.00. SP: but not in rooms.

Renowned reputation. A must for many cyclists who enjoy atmosphere,
hospitality and all-round comfort. Fine ales and huge helpings of tasty food.
Camra & Good Pub Guide.

THE OLD SCHOOL HOUSE,
Helen Ratcliffe & Alan Smith, Allenheads,
Hexham, Northumberland, NE47 9HR
T: 01434 685040
E: helenheads@aol.com
W: www.acart.org.uk
R: 2 rooms each with 4 bunk beds
B&B: £18. EM: £10-£15.

A friendly and interesting place. "Superb dinner and tremendous breakfast, best so far on route." "Great atmosphere, unrivalled views." (Quotes from C2C'ers). Home of Allenheads Contemporary Arts, it often presents exhibitions of artists working in the rural community of Allenheads.

ALLENHEADS LODGE, Allenheads,
Northumberland NE47 9HW
T: 0191 567 8647
F: 0191 514 4947
E: allenheadslodge@springboard-ne.org
W: www.web.springboard-ne.org
R: 4 (Total of 22 beds)
B&B: £18.80. EM: On request. PL: £4.

Pub 400m. Central heating, secure bike lock-up, drying room, separate showers.

NEW HOUSES B&B,
Pat & Terry McMullon,
Allenheads,
Hexham,
Northumberland NE47 9HX
T/F: 01434 685 260
E: zookon@aol.com
R: 1S, 2T. B&B: £20-£25. PL: £3.50.
Warm, spacious and very comfortable cottage with all amenities. Walking distance to pub.

Across the Durham moors - a still point in time

ROOKHOPE

The stretch out of Allenheads is almost the last tortuous ascent – but it does seem to drag on until you reach the summit at Currick. Then there is a nice stretch of gentle downhill all the way to Rookhope. You soon pass the boundary into County Durham, land of the Prince Bishops – palatinate rulers with absolute authority equal to a sovereign within the principality. They were granted such power because of the strategic importance of the area in the ongoing battle with the Scots.

On your approach you will pass the Lintzgarth Arch, an incongruous and enormous vestige of a bygone era lying abandoned on the valley floor. The arch carried a 3km horizontal chimney across the valley which replaced the more conventional vertical type when it was realised that a lot of lead literally went up with the smoke. Consequently teams of chimneysweeps were employed to scrape the valuable lead and silver deposits from the chimney once a week. It was a dangerous and filthy job done by children.

Rookhope is another shrunken mining village. It is also charming, keeping the secret of its hiding place well guarded from sight high above the Weardale Valley. It is hard to imagine that this small group of dwellings was a hive of activity only a few years ago.

In its heyday it supported a surgery, a resident district nurse, vicar, policeman, teashops, several crowded pubs and a busy school. The mining of lead, iron and fluorspar, smelting and the railways totally dominated people's lives.

Today the village is a welcome watering hole and resting place for weary cyclists before the final leg of the C2C journey down to the NE coast. Now there is only a pub (newly refurbished), village shop, post office and working man's club - but a splendid stopping off point, nonetheless.

THE ROOKHOPE INN,
Chris Jones & Alan Jackson,
Rookhope, Weardale,
Co. Durham DL13 2BG
T: 01388 517215. F: 01388 517861
E: spottydoggy1@hotmail.com
W: www.rookhope.com
R: 1D, 3T, 1F
B&B: £25. EM: £4.50-£6.
PL: £3.50

On route, 'soopa doopa' drying facilities.
Restored 300 year old village inn which especially welcomes cyclists. En-suite accommodation, good food, live music. (SEE AD ON P. 168)

THE OLD VICARAGE, Colin & Pauline Lomas,
1 Stotsfield Burn, Rookhope in Weardale, Co.
Durham, DL13 2AF
T: 01388 517 375: 01388 517 701
E: colin@finetime.fsbusiness.co
R: 1T, 2F. B&B: £20. EM: £9.50 (3 courses + coffee
& vegetarian). PL: £3.50

Pub 500m. Large detached stone-built house in
own secluded, tranquil grounds, orchard garden & courtyard seating to relax in. Spacious rooms with tea and coffee-making facilities. Known for 'comfort, excellent food and generous hospitality', according to our visitors book. Large lounge, log fire, TV/Video/DVD. Reading selection. Board games.

STANHOPE

From Rookhope you can take the exciting but demanding off-road section which climbs steeply past ruins and heads along the edge of Edmundbyers Common, leading down to the Waskerley Way either by road or across a track – the choice is yours.

The second option is to go via Stanhope, one of Weardale's more important and historic little market towns. But if you go this way, remember that you'll be facing a swine of a climb up the B6278 to the Waskerley Way, aptly called Crawleyside.

Originally a Bronze Age settlement, it was a tiny village around a cobbled market square until the Stanhope & Tyne Railway was built to transport the industrial produce to Consett and Cleveland along the Waskerley Way. Before the railways, all raw materials were transported by pack horses. Teams of tough little Galloway horses would pick their way over the Pennines and then down into the valleys, the lead horse often having a bell attached to his harness to guide the following horses across the mist-cloaked moors.

CYCLE SHOPS
The Bike Shop, Terry & Lorraine Turnbull at Mile Post 100 at the start of the Waskerley Way, 5km from Stanhope. 01388 526434.

PLACES OF INTEREST
Durham Dales Visitor Centre, Castle Gardens. Café. 01388 527 650
Fossilised tree at St Thomas's Church, 350 million years old, found in 1914 in an Edmundbyers mine
St Thomas's Church, 12th century origins complete with Roman altar and Saxon font.

EATING OUT

Queen's Head Hotel, Front St. Good pub fare, reasonable price.
01388 528160.
The Bike Stop, stamping post & great teas. Mile post 100
Various pubs. All in town centre

QUEEN'S HEAD HOTEL,
John Emerson & Carol Pattillo,
89 Front Street, Stanhope, Weardale, DL13 2UB
T/F: 01388 528160
E: <u>queenshead-stanhope@yahoo.co.uk</u>
W: <u>www.queenshead_stanhope.co.uk</u>
R: 4T. B&B: £23-£30.

EM: £3-£7   PL: Priced per item. Hotel has public bar. A small, friendly local
pub with bar and dining room, stocking an ever-changing selection of real
ales.

REDLODGE GUEST HOUSE,
Pauline Sorensen, 2 Market Place,
Stanhope, DL13 2UN
T: 01388 527 851
E: <u>redlodgegh@hotmail.com</u>
W: <u>www.redlodgeh.co.uk</u>
R: 1S, 2T (E-S).
B&B: £25. On route, 50m from pub.
Old stone house in centre of town. Central heating, pleasant rooms,
bathroom with bath & shower facilities. Lounge/dining room for guests to
enjoy. All facilities on the doorstep.

JUBILEE ADVENTURE CENTRE,
Pam Welford, Crawleyside,
nr Stanhope, Weardale,
Co Durham.
T: 0191 384 9266.
Dormitories. 42 beds. See ad on p.165

CONSETT

Whether you are coming via Edmunbyers Common **(see display box for YHA)** or Stanhope, you will shortly be passing the 100 mile point stamping station at the Bike Stop at the start of the Waskerley Way. You can get spares and repairs here, or tea and cake, plus overnight bunkhouse or B&B accommodation **(see display box)**. And it's all down hill from here.

This is a pleasant and easy section of the route, past Muggleswick Common, Waskerley and Smiddy Shaw reservoirs, followed by a quick canter into Park Head Plantation near Bee Cottage, and down to the A68. Beyond here is the magnificent Hownsgill Viaduct which carried the Stanhope and Tyne Railway Line, Britain's first commercial railway route. There are great views from here across sweeping tracts of deciduous forest and undulating landscape, on the edge of an area that was once the embodiment of heavy British industry. The pathway is dotted with imaginative Sustrans signage and sculptures cast from industrial relics.

PARKHEAD STATION BUNKHOUSE
B&B AND TEA ROOMS,
Terry & Lorraine Turnbull,
Stanhope Moor, Stanhope,
Co Durham, DL13 2ES
T: 01388 526434

E: parkheadstation@aol.com
R: 3D, 1F, 1S (E-S) (Disabled Access).
Bunkhouse sleeps 8. Prices: B&B £25 per person per night, bunkhouse
prices available on request.
EM: yes. PL: yes.
Adjacent C2C cycle route/Waskerley Way, perfect for family cycling and
walking. Enjoy the panoramic views from the one-time station master's
house, where a warm welcome awaits you.

*Just four miles along the B6278 from Parkhead is the lovely old YHA at
Edmundbyers, originally an inn dating from 1600. If is a slight diversion, but
you can rejoin the route following the lane just beyond Consett. Very close to
Beamish*

EDMUNBYERS YHA,
The manager,
Low House,
Edmunbyers,
Consett, Co. Durham, DH8 9NL
T: 0870 7705810 or 01207 255651

E: edmundbyers@yha.org.uk
W: www.yha.org.uk
R: 6 - 1Tpl, 1Q, 2 (5), 2 (6).
Price: £11 adult, £8 for u-18. Self-catering only.
Wonderful beamed ceilings and cosy open fire, the centre has been
comfortably and sensitively refurbished.
Worth the detour - a memorable place to stay. Former inn. Close to
Beamish and also the scenic village of Blanchland.
Quarter of a mile from Derwent Reservoir.

BEE COTTAGE FARMHOUSE B&B,
David & Melita Turner, Castleside,
Consett, Co Durham, DH8 9HW
T: 01207 508224
R: 2D, 2T, 4F. B&B £29-£40. EM: £16.50 (3-courses + coffee). PL: £6.
4 diamonds. Stunning views, Leave C2C at

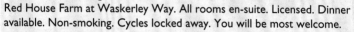

Red House Farm at Waskerley Way. All rooms en-suite. Licensed. Dinner available. Non-smoking. Cycles locked away. You will be most welcome.
W: www.beecottage.co.uk
E: welcome@beecottagefarmhouse.freeserve.co.uk

ST IVES, Sandra Tilney,
22 St Ives Rd., Leadgate, Consett, Co Durham, DH8 7PY
T: 01207 580173
R: 2Tpl. B&B: £25 pppn. EM: no. PL: £4.
New establishment. Pubs just a few minutes away.
Comfortable, modernised old house on the main road bang next to the route. Ideal stop-off, with en-suite rooms and a big breakfast to boost you next day. Real welcome fpr cyclists.

Just before Consett are the Terris Novalis sculptures, which overlook the 700 acre site of what was once the mighty Consett Steelworks. The Turner prize winning works – a stainless steel theodolite and an engineer's level by Tony Cragg – are nearly 7m tall, are 20 times life size, and symbolise regeneration in an area convulsed by the death of heavy industry towards the end of the last century. The art works were commissioned by Sustrans and will stand as a monument to this admirable body long after the combustion engine has had its day.

"The work sited at Consett marks the watershed between the upland/moorland landscape and the extremes of the Industrial Age," says the Sustrans website. "Local people see this landmark as a monument to the scale of local industry and its demise – the tragedy that has followed."

Cast iron waysigns flutter in the breeze under the gaze of pylons and transformers

PLACES OF INTEREST
Shotley Bridge - an old spa town, well-known for German sword-makers in the 17th century.

EATING OUT
Grey Horse, real ales brewed on the premises. Light lunches and right on C2C route.

Jolly Drovers Pub Leadgate 01207 503 994

C2C Features: dotted along the line are story-boards set on vertical sleepers which interpret the history of the railway. These are chapters taken from a novel, The Celestial Railroad, by John Downie. It is available from Sustrans North Eastern Office at Stanley, 01207 281 259.

CYCLE SHOPS
Consett Cycle Co, 62 Medomsley Rd 01207 581 205
McVickers Sports, Front Street 01207 505 121
MOTECH, 62/64 Medomsley Road 01207 581205

At Consett the routes part company for the final time; one goes to Sunderland and the other to Newcastle. The original route end was into Sunderland, so I shall deal with this one first. From Consett you head for Stanley, but first you have to get out of Consett so pay heed to the signs.

Go round the A692 roundabout , briefly up the left side of Front St before going left between Edith Street and Albert Rd. Cross the latter half way up and go right into Park Rd, cross Front St before heading left and across the B6308, then the path takes you thourgh Leadgate and past the Annfield Plain. Look out for the Kyo Undercurrents sculpture – a series of earth and stone ramps.

STANLEY

Stanley is set on a breezy hill top and commands a bird's eye view of the whole area. Sustrans North Eastern Office is here so if you have any positive or negative feedback on the route, write to them at Rockwood House, Barn Hill, Stanley, Co. Durham DH9 8AN. David Gray, the man largely responsible for the past 100-odd miles of fun and pain, will be the recipient. Information on other Sustrans Bike Routes is available here together with cycle literature and C2C T-shirts (you can also join the Sustrans Charity if you are not already a member).

EATING OUT

Hill Top Restaurant   East Street 01207 233 217
Shafto's Bar   Causey Farm 01207 235 555

PLACES OF INTEREST

Beamish Museum is England's largest open-air museum and has a working steam railway, trams, a Victorian town centre, a demonstration colliery, a school and a working farm. The C2C route passes within yards of the entrance gate.
Tanfield Railway: the oldest railway in the world that still exists. It stops at the Causey Arch north of Stanley – 50m high and a Scheduled Ancient Monument built in 1728 – and is manned by volunteers 0191 274 2002.
Jolly Drovers Maze – built on the site of the former Eden Pit Colliery in 1989. Like the Lambton Worm (see Chester-le-Street) it was designed by Andy Goldsworthy.

THE BIKE BUS *(see ad on page 166)*
The Bus Station, Stanley, Co Durham, DH9 0TD
Tel: 01207 237424
E: bike.bus@btconnect.com
W: www.minicoachhire.co.uk
Cyclist and Bike Transport specialists. Transported throughout the U.K.
Size of group no object. Very competitive rates.

BEAMISH MARY INN,
Graham Ford,
No Place, Stanley,
Co. Durham DH9 0QH
T: 0191 370 0237 F: 0191 370 0091
E: beamishmary@hotmail.co.uk
W: www.beamishmary.com
R: 4D. B&B <£25. EM: <£4.00
DFR: 800m. 3 diamonds.

Traditional Inn. Specialises in good food, real ale, live music. Comfortable
atmosphere. All rooms en-suite, 1 with private bath. Cyclists/walkers most
welcome.

CHESTER-LE-STREET

Just follow the transformed transformers. Not quite the Stanley
Sphnixes, these great steel monoliths, sculpted from reclaimed scraps,
have nonetheless assumed iconic status. Don't forget to look at the
metal cows (*page 89*) near Beamish. Created by Sally Matthews, they
are surprisingly graceful as they stand beside the path, turning grass
into rust.

There's also King Coal by artist David Kemp, next to the abandoned
railway line at Pelton Fell. This was built of stone from the dismantled
Consett railway station bridge, bricks from old kilns and British Coal
provided the crown. It was put together by a stonemason and local
volunteers and was, by sheer coincidence, finished on October 15 1992
– the very day of the announcement of the closure of the last pits in
Durham coalfields.

Consett: The Terris Novalis sculptures by Tony Cragg, a former winner of the Turner Prize

Chester-le-Street is the oldest town in County Durham, and was once a Roman settlement. The Washington Wildfowl and Wetlands Centre is very near the route. This 100-acre waterfowl park designed by Peter Scott has over 1,200 birds and is visited by several mammals including the scarce water vole.

MALLING GUEST HOUSE, Heather Rippon,
1 Oakdale Terrace, Newfield, Chester-le-Street, DH2 2SU
T: 0191 370 2571
E: heather@mallingguesthouse.freeserve.co.uk
W: www.mallingguesthouse.freeserve.co.uk
R: 1S, 1T, 1F. B&B: £25-£34. PL: approx. £4
DFR: 300m.
Pub opposite . 3 diamonds. Friendly, experienced proprietors, the house has lovely westward views from the conservatory. For the last 14 years we have been welcoming cyclists.

PLACES OF INTEREST
The Washington Wetlands Trust, 100 acres of magnificent parkland, ponds and hides 0191 416 5454

EATING OUT
The Wheatsheaf, Pelaw Grange 0191 388 3104
The Barley Mow, Browns Buildings 0191 410 4504

CYCLE SHOPS
Cestria Cycles, 11 Ashfield Terrace - 0191 388 7535
C2C Features: the Penshaw Monument, a look-alike Doric Temple dedicated to Theseus, was built in memory of John George Lambton, the 1st Earl of Durham.

Be thankful to leave the river here for fear of the Lambton Worm. The legend runs that a young Lambton lad, fishing in the river against all advice, caught a small worm. In disgust he threw it into a nearby well and went off to fight in the Crusades. On his return the "worm" had grown into a dragon which ravaged the countryside. A witch agreed to slay the beast on condition that Lambton kill the first living thing he met. Unfortunately it was his father, whom of course he spared, and so failed to fulfil his side of the bargain, thus nine generations of Lambtons were condemned to meet untimely ends.

SUNDERLAND

The last leg of the route is scenic as it follows the north bank of the Wear, skirting Washington and passing the Stadium of Light. This route opened three years ago and is reasonably easy to follow. The end is at the Marina at Roker. This is a grand spot to finish. Tradition has it that you dip your wheel in the briny just like at the start.

Sunderland, once home of shipbuilding, coal-mining, glass blowing and rope making, became a city in 1992 and is just a stone's throw from the coast and the North Sea. St Peter's Church, built in 674 when Sunderland became established as one of England's earliest centres

Victoria Viaduct, on the outskirts of Sunderland, at dusk.

of Christianity, was notable as the first "glazed" building in England. This was once one of the most important shipbuilding towns in the world and you can still clearly see where the old shipyards were from the Wearmouth Bridge. George Washington's ancestral home is in Washington village, which is now part of the city of Sunderland: what an amazing connection with Whitehaven, the start of the C2C, where Washington's grandparents had their home.

PLACES OF INTEREST

Washington Old Hall, Washington village. George Washington's ancestral home 0191 416 6879.

National Glass Centre, demonstration of glass blowing plus the **Throwing Stones Restaurant**

Crowtree Leisure Centre, town centre 0191 553 2600

St Peter's Church, one of the oldest churches in Britain with a Saxon wall dating back to 674.

St Andrew's Church, Roker Victorian centre of William Morris' arts & craft movement.

Sunderland Museum & Winter Gardens, The Sunderland Story – shipbuilding etc. 0191 553 2323

Wearmouth Bridge, impressive early 19th century construction. Some great views.

King Coal by artist David Kemp. Reminder of the grim end of an old industry

CYCLE SHOPS

Peter Darke Cycles	113 High St West, 0191 510 8155
Cycle World	222 High St West 0191 514 1974
The Big Bike Shop	214 High St West 0191 567 9090

USEFUL INFO

Tourist Information Centre	Fawcett St. 0191 553 2000/1/2
Early closing	Wednesday
Sunderland Royal Hospital,	Kayll Rd. 0191 565 6256

BRENDON PARK, Angela & Jimmy Carter,
49 Roker Park Road, Roker, Sunderland SR6 9PL
T: 0191 548 9303.
E: brendonpark@rokerguesthouse.co.uk
R: 1D, 1T, 4F (E-S available)
B&B: <£18.00. PL: £3.75 (by request)
DFR: 500m. Pub nearby. 3 diamonds. Near Marine Centre and Seaburn Railway Station. Clean, comfortable, spacious rooms with TV, tea/coffee making-facilities. Ideal for weary travellers.

NEWCASTLE

The Newcastle route follows the Derwent Walk. This takes you through Hamsterley Mill, Rowland's Gill and then some pretty, landscaped areas by the river Derwent. When you get to the Tyne go left, over the bridge to the Hadrian's Way path. Although you start off on an industrial stretch, you are soon back beside the river.

The ride along the Quayside is one of the high points for me. It follows the start of the Coast & Castles route, and the route description which follows borrows heavily from my guide book to that magnificent ride from Newcastle to Edinburgh (Coast & Castles - The Complete Guide). I make no apologies.

Newcastle is one of the most 'happening' places in northern Europe. A magnet for shoppers and clubbers, diners and drinkers, it boasts some of Britain's finest architecture and has gone through a cultural Renaissance. Recent restoration projects have included Norman fortifications, 16th century merchant houses and the great neo-classical designs of Grainger Town. There are also art galleries, museums and concert venues aplenty.

Newcastle and Gateshead, its neighbour on the south bank of the Tyne, have been voted England's best short break destination. The two towns also teamed up to contend for the European Capital of Culture in 2008, a link symbolised by the arcing strand of the new Gateshead Millennium Bridge across the Tyne. Sadly, the gong went to a town arguably in greater need of culture: Liverpool.

The final leg: along Newcastle's rejuvenated Quayside

PLACES OF INTEREST

Castle Keep, Castle Garth, St Nicholas St 0191 232 7938: Built by Henry II between 1168-78 on the site of the so-called New Castle *(left)*, it was after this edifice that the town was named. The New Castle itself was constructed on the site of the Roman Pons Aelius (Bridge of Hadrian). Admission: £1.50, 50p concessions.

BALTIC The Centre for Contemporary Art *(left)*, Gateshead Quays 0191 478 1810 Opened in July 2002, BALTIC is the major new centre for contemporary visual art and stands grandly above the water on the south bank. Five galleries and more than 3,000 square metres.

Gateshead Millennium Bridge. Takes walkers and cyclists from Newcastle's Quayside across to Gateshead Quays and BALTIC Square. The bridge opens and closes like an eyelid, allowing shipping to pass. Like many of the revellers, it is spectacularly lit at night.

Grainger Town – a rejuvenated architectural treasure containing Many of the city's top shops *(see Central Station above left)*.

Chinatown – around Stowell St. Restaurant standard is good and prices reasonable.

The Sage Gateshead, Gateshead Quays opening 2005. Sir Norman Foster's contribution to the Geordie quayside, a music complex catering for classical, folk, jazz, brass and choral. Until then, music events are handled from The Sage at Gateshead Town Hall 0191 443 4666 or 0870 7034555 for the box office.

WHERE TO STAY?

There are plenty of hotels and guest houses. The Jesmond area, just north of the centre, is full of places to stay and lively night spots. If you're overnighting in the city, there are hotels near the waterfront, down on the fashionable **Quayside**. For a full list of hotels, call the **Tourist Information Centre** on 0191 277 8000 or get hold of the **Newcastle Gateshead Accommodation Guide** ngi@ngi.org.uk by calling the **Newcastle Gateshead Initiative** on 0191 243 8800.

Premier Lodge, The Exchange, Quayside. Rooms £49.95. 0870 990 6530.
Travelodge, 4 Forster St, Quayside. All 120 rooms £63. Family room will sleep three if the double bed is shared! 0191 261 5432
Youth Hostel, 107 Jesmond Rd. 0191 281 2570
£11.40 for under-18. £14.65 for over-18. Members only, but non-members can join up on arrival. *(see ad on p .164)*
The George Hotel, 88 Osborne Rd, Jesmond. 0191 281 4442/2943
Small family run concern with 16 rooms. From £35.
Kenilworth Hotel, 44 Osborne Rd, Jesmond. 0191 281 8111
Family business run by keen cyclist. 12 bedroom from £38.
Da Vinci's, 73 Osborne Rd, Jesmond. Good, cheap wildly Italian restaurant with 15 bedrooms from £40. 0191 281 5284
Westland Hotel, 27 Osborne Avenue, Jesmond. Friendly, family run hotel. Secure area for cycles. 14 bedrooms from £25 a night. 0191 281 0412

The stretch of Quayside from the Millennium Bridge is known as the 'Golden Mile of Culture' on both banks, because of the number of galleries, museums and concert venues.

Head due east along the Tyne, past the law courts, smart hotels, wine bars and riverside apartments, where new Geordie money flaunts itself. Beyond there, as the river loops past Byker and round towards Wallsend, towards the shipyards and the giant cranes, the old Tyneside re-emerges. It's goodbye to the metropolis, with its acres of glass and stainless steel, and hello to fine relics of a recently bygone age.

TYNEMOUTH – THE END OF THE ROAD

There are 60s high rise flats and men in cloth caps walking whippets and tending pigeon lofts. The route (marked C2C and 72) leads continuously along the north bank, past the Segedunum Roman Fort, to the end of the Hadrian's Wall National Trail.

WALLSEND is ideal for the Hadrian's Wall experience. The fort at Segedunum was recently brought back to life at a cost of £9 million, and displays the only Roman bath-house in Britain.

A couple of miles down river on the opposite bank sits Jarrow, home of the Venerable Bede, and the Bede's World Museum. It was also the starting point for the Jarrow March. Two hundred hunger strikers descended upon London in 1936 and made one of the most striking political statements in British working class history.

As you approach the Royal Quays North Sea Ferry Terminus make sure you follow the signs (easily missed) and go to the LEFT of the Wet 'n' Wild water centre (you can't miss it – the giant flume tubes look like part of some space-age factory). Follow the path through landscaped public gardens in which an incongruous cluster of wooden sea groynes stand, as if awaiting tidal erosion. Turn left just beyond them, by a faded waysign – do not head back in the direction of the Amsterdam and Bergen ferry terminal – and go through the modern housing estate. To the right, pleasure craft and fishing boats should be bobbing around at their moorings.

Keep following the C2C, Route 72 and Route 10 signs (they are clustered together) and you will find yourself passing through another modern housing estate. You are now in North Shields, erstwhile home of comedian Stan Laurel.

Following the signs, descend a steep flight of stone steps to the fish quays. You will arrive outside a pub called the Chain Locker, opposite the ferry terminus to South Shields. The view across the Tyne on a good day is worth a pause. You can see, in the far distance, the elegant 19th century façade of the clock tower of South Shields town hall.

Cafes, stores and splendid fish & chip restaurants run the length of the North Shields Quays. This is where Danish and Polish sailors used to integrate vigorously with the local community at a den of iniquity called the Infamous Jungle, now known as the Collingwood Buildings.

You soon round the point where the North Sea meets the Tyne. Welcome to Tynemouth. You pass the 11th century Priory and Castle, and the handsome statue of the man who really won the Battle of Trafalgar in 1805, Admiral Lord Collingwood. Nelson's unassuming and undersung deputy single-handedly took on five French warships for a full hour before the rest of the English fleet caught up. He assumed command upon Nelson's death half-way through the battle, and is Tynemouth's most famous son.

This is a stylish little haven centred upon Front St, a handsome wide avenue built for eating, drinking and promenading. The village is a conservation area of architectural gems from the 18th and 19th centuries. The stretch of shore from here, through Cullercoats and up to Whitley Bay, is known as Newcastle's Côte d'Azur. You will note that there is cycle parking in Tynemouth and Whitley Bay, just over a mile up the coast.

This is where you finish, though there is no obvious place to crack a bottle of Evian Water. No matter. It is a delightful spot and there is bags of accommodation in Whitley Bay, just round the corner (plus a couple of B&Bs in Tynemouth itself).

Don't forget to dip your front wheel in the water.

PLACES TO EAT

Sidneys, Percy Park Rd.Now features in Michelin. 0191 257 8500
Giorgio's Pizzeria & Restaurant, Front St. 0191 257 3758
Marshall's Fryery at the Priory, Front St. 0191 257 2435
The Gate of India, 40 Front St. 0191 258 3453
Gibraltar Rock, Carvery East St. 0191 258 5655

THE END

There are several good pubs in Tynemouth. Here are three recommendations learned from bitter experience. Forgive the pun...

Tynemouth Lodge Hotel, Tynemouth Rd, a real locals pub frequented by the lifeboatmen. Great beers and often very busy. It's at the top of that steep climb out of the North Shields fish quays, on the edge of

Tynemouth. Worth tracking back if you have got the energy.
Fitzpatricks, Front Street, is a handsome establishment. It is one of
eight pubs in the small town. Has a changing selection of hand-pulled
ales. Food served.

The Turks Head, Front St., otherwise known as the Stuffed Dog
because of Willie the Scottish collie, whose 130 year old taxidermised
remains sit in a glass box looking at the bar. Willie came down
from the Scottish Borders with a herd of sheep and a shepherd, but
somehow got separated from them and spent the rest of his life waiting
and pining in Tynemouth for his lost master. A tale of epic proportions
told in detail on a plaque. Good Courage Directors, regular guest ales.
Food served all day.

Whitley Bay and Tynemouth adjoin each other so are equally
suitable for that final night. It is impossible not to notice that this
resort, with its Pleasure Dome, Spanish City and seaside villas, is
geared up for tourism and little else. Every other building offers
food, drink or accommodation – or all three. Whitley Bay is a striking
seaside resort, and in the past was a thriving holiday resort for tourists.
It is currently attempting to rediscover its former glory, when smart
Geordies would jockey for position on Newcastle Coast's promenade.

MARLBOROUGH HOTEL,
Hilary & Allen Thompson
20-21 East Parade,
Promenade, Whitley Bay, NE26 1AP
T: 0191 251 3628
F: 0191 252 5033
E: reception@marlborough-hotel.com
W: www.marlborough-hotel.com
B&B: £25 - £35. R: 4S, 6D, 2T, 4F. PL: £5. SP
4 diamonds. Sea front family run hotel in prime position on Whitley Bay.
High standards of hospitality and accommodation. Close to transport links

YORK HOUSE HOTEL,
Michael & Marissa Ruddy
106-110 Park Avenue,
Whitley Bay, NE26 1DN
T: 0191 252 8313 F: 0191 251 3953
E: reservations@yorkhousehotel.com
W: www.yorkhousehotel.com
Rooms: 5D, 2S, 3T, 3F. B&B: £27.50 - £32.50. EM: No. PL: £5.95. SP in
some areas. 4 diamonds. Near route and 100m from pub.
Delightful family run hotel. Conveniently yet quietly situated close to all
amenities. 250 metres from beach. All rooms are en-suite with fridges and
microwaves

AVALON HOTEL,
Michael Farwell,
26-28 South Parade,
Whitley Bay, Tyne & Wear NE26 2RG
T: 0191 251 0080 F: 0191 251 0100
E: reception@avalon-hotel.freeserve.co.uk
W: www.avalon-hotel.freeserve.co.uk
B&B: £35 - £55. R: 4S, 4D, 7T, 1F. 2-star.
EM: £5.00-£10.00. PL: Yes. SP. Next door to pub. Near start/end of route.
Family run; all rooms en-suite; secure bike parking; full licence; restaurant;
new owners; washing & drying facilities.

CAMPING & CARAVAN SITES

WORKINGTON
Inglenook Caravan & Camping Park,
Fitz Bridge, Lamplugh, Workington, CA14 4SH (on C2C) 4 Star
Camping Park.
01946 861240

BRAITHWAITE
Scotgate Chalet, Camping & Caravan Holiday Park,
Braithwaite, Keswick, Cumbria CA12 5TF (C2C 100 yds) T/F:
017687 78343/ 78099

PENRUDDOCK
Beckses Caravan & Camping Park,
Penruddock, Penrith, Cumbria CA11 0RX (1km from C2C)
017684 83224

ALSTON
Horse & Waggon Camping & Caravan Park,
Nentsberry, Alston, Cumbria CA9 3LH, William Patterson (swings
on play area, WC and showers available, 3 miles south-east Alston on
A689. Tents from £4.00, OS map ref NY 764 451)
01434 382 805

HAMSTERLEY
Byreside Caravan Site,
Hamsterley, Newcastle-upon-Tyne NE17 7RT, Mrs Val Clemitson,
between Ebchester and Hamsterley Mill, adjacent to Derwent Walk
Cycle Track.
01207 560280/560499

BEAMISH
Bobby Shafto Caravan Park,
Beamish, Co. Durham DH9 0RY (adjacent to world famous Beamish
Museum, only ¾ mile from C2C route).
T: 0191 370 1776

YOUTH HOSTELS

YHA Head Office
Northern Region, PO Box 11, Matlock, Derbyshire
DE4 3YH (inc SAE)
0870 770 8868.

Cockermouth Youth Hostel,
Double Mills, Cockermouth, Cumbria CA13 ODS.
£6.50 (u-18s) £9.0. On route.
0870 770 5768

Skiddaw House Youth Hostel
Bassenthwaite, Keswick, Cumbria CA12 4QX.
£5.50 (u-18s) £8.00 (adults), self-catering only.
07801 207 401

Keswick Youth Hostel,
Station Road, Keswick, Cumbria CA12 5LH.
£8.25 (u-18s) £11.50.
Membership requirement: available at Hostel.
(on C2C route)
0870 770 5894

Alston Youth Hostel,
The Firs, Alston,
Cumbria CA9 3RW.
£7.00 (u-18s) £10.25.
0870 770 5668

Edmundbyers Youth Hostel,
Low House, Edmundbyers,
Consett, Co Durham DH8 9NL.
£6.50 (under 18s) £9. On route.
T/F: 0870 770 5810

Newcastle upon Tyne Youth Hostel,
107 Jesmond Road,
Newcastle upon Tyne NE2 1NJ.
£8.25 (under 18s) £11.50.
0870 7705 972 _(see p.164)_

CAMPING BARNS

Camping Barns are stone barns providing simple overnight shelter. They are roomy and dry, so there is no need to carry a tent. They have a wooden sleeping platform sometimes with mattresses. Tables, a slate cooking bench and cold water tap and WC are also provided together with a washing-up bowl, clothes hooks and waste bags.

CUMBRIA

For bookings at most of the Lake District National Park barns you must first ring Keswick Information Centre on 017687 72645

Loweswater - Swallow Barn, Waterend Farm (west end of Loweswater, on C2C route) <u>OS NY 116 226</u>.
Newlands Valley - Catbells Barn, (c. 2 miles from C2C route) <u>OS NY 243 208.</u>
Keswick - Tarn Flatt Barn, Sandwith (4 miles from Whitehaven) OS <u>NX 947 146.</u>
Mungrisdale - Blake Beck Barn between Keswick and Penrith, (c. 2 miles from C2C route) <u>OS NY 367 278</u>.

USEFUL TELEPHONE NUMBERS

WEATHER NEWS
Lake District National Park Weather Line 017687 75757
Weathercheck 09001 333111

TOURIST INFORMATION CENTRES

Whitehaven 01946 852 939
Keswick 017687 72 645
Cockermouth 01900 822 634
Penrith 01768 867 466
Alston (April to October) 01434 382244
Stanhope 01388 527 650

Beamish 0191 370 4000
Gateshead 0191 433 8420
Sunderland 0191 553 2000
Newcastle upon Tyne 0191 261 0610
Whitley Bay 0191 200 8535

TRAVEL INFORMATION: BUS, COACH AND TRAIN

Stagecoach NW 0870 608 2608
Durham County Council Travellink 0191 383 3337
National Express 08705 808080
National Express Newcastle 08705 808080
National Rail Enquiries Line 08457484950
Scotrail Enquiries Line 08457 550033
Cycle Booking Line NW Trains 0845 604 0231

BIKE SHOPS AND REPAIRS

Whitehaven

**Haven Cycles - hire & repair, Preston St
Garage** 01946 632633
Dave Milling, Preston St
01946 63380

Workington

New Bike Shop, 18-20 Market Pl
01900 603 337

Cockermouth **Derwent Cycles, 4 Market Place**
01900 822 113
4-Play Cycles, 25 Market Place
01900 823377

Braithwaite

Bike Repairs, Ian Hindmarch
017687 78273

Keswick

Keswick Mountain Bikes, Southey Hill
017687 75202

| Penrith | **Arragons, 2 Brunswick Rd** 01768 890 344 |
| | **Harpers, 1-2 Middlegate** 01768 864 475 |

Nenthead   **Mark Fearn, blacksmith** 01434 382194

Allenheads   **Village Shop: essential bike spares**

Stanhope   The Bike Shop, Waskerley Way, 5km from
Stanhope. 01388 526434.

Consett   **Motech Cycle Co, 62 Medomsley Rd**
01207 581 205

Stanley   **Main Brothers, Front St** 01207 290258

Chester-le-St   **Cestria Cycles, 11 Ashfield Terrace**
0191 388 7535

Washington   **Houghton Cycles & Outdoor Leisure,**
3 West View 0191 416 9906

Metro Centre   **The Bike Place, Market Lane, Swallwell**
0191 488 3137

Newcastle   **Edinburgh Bicycle Co-operative,**
5 Union Rd, Byker
0191 265 8619

Sunderland   **Darke Cycles, 1 William St** 0191 510 8155
Cycle World, 222 High St West
0191 565 8188

Part II

THE REIVERS GUIDE

A Cycle Route from Tynemouth to Whitehaven

MAPS

Though I provide some basic mapping and there is some waymarking, you should take the official route map available from Footprint for £4.50 (01786 479866 or **www.footprintmaps.co.uk**), Sustrans (0117 929 0888) or Cordee Books & Maps (01162 543579 **www.cordee. co.uk**). OS Landranger maps (1:50,000) 88, 87, 80, 79, 86, 85, 90 & 89 (in sequence for east to west). If you don't mind bulk and cost, the new Landranger will furnish you with full route details (N.B. older ones will not have Route 10 marked on them).

INTRODUCTION

The Reivers Route opened in 1998 and is 173 miles long. It is also known as the 'Return C2C' as it takes you from the end all the way back to the start of the C2C. But it is a great route in its own right – in some ways superior to the C2C. However it has not had as much attention and money spent on it, and is not a fully fledged Sustrans route, so is not given the mile-by-mile care of the C2C.

Indeed some who live along the way are concerned that not enough is being done to push this beautiful and isolated stretch of northern wilderness.

Well, I have some news for you all: a cycle route management unit has been set up to work closely local authorities along its entire length. There will be full co-operation with Sustrans and a concerted effort to manage and market Reivers as part of the overall North East Cycle Tourism Strategy.

As with the C2C the gradients along Reivers work in the cyclist's favour. The route winds its way through some of the wildest and most untouched countryside in the UK from the mouth of the mighty River Tyne to the Cumbrian coast. Along the way riders will follow the shores of Kielder Water – Europe's largest man-made lake – before crossing the border for a brief foray into Scotland.

Emerging from the post-industrial and partially regenerated suburbs of Newcastle, the route quickly threads its way into the first gentle then rugged countryside of the Northumberland National Park. There are fine views across to the towering Cheviots before you become immersed in the forest tracks around Keilder, where there are many options suited to mountain bikers and day tripper alike. After the Borders, Carlisle then the Lake District.

This is truly isolated terrain. You could be up in the fastnesses of Sutherland or Ross. But unlike up there, you stumble across such gems as Hesket Newmarket, with its own excellent micro-brewery, Newcastleton just over the Scottish border, or Cockermouth and Bassenthwaite. There is a great deal of satisfaction to be had from such discoveries.

BLOOD & GUTS: THE HISTORY

As you will probably know, the word Reiver means plunderer. The route is named after the murdering bandits who ran a medieval equivalent of Cosa Nostra. This was the Chicago or Sicily of its time, when marauding clans terrorised the English and Scottish Borders for 350 years, until the 17th century. They lived by cattle rustling, kidnapping, extortion, arson and murder.

The route passes many fortified farmhouses revealing the defensive needs of the area as well as its rich heritage. Despite the cosy thematising perpetrated by tourism to give the past a false appeal, there is nothing remotely quaint or even honourable about Reiving; many of the families were happy to swing both ways, fighting for the English if the price was right, or vice versa. One family, the Grahams, were so infamous that their surnames were banned by law, so the Grahams changed them to Maharg (Graham backwards), which later also became McHarg.

Indeed, the word 'blackmail' comes from the Reivers: a farmer paid 'black-mail' – rent in the form of cattle instead of the legal 'white-rent', which was paid in silver, to a powerful Reiver who would give him 'protection' in return.

HERE I GIVE YOU A FULL LIST OF THE GUILTY FAMILY NAMES:

Archbold; Armstrong; Beattie; Bell; Burns; Carleton; Carlisle; Carnaby; Carrs; Carruthers; Chamberlain; Charlton; Collingwood; Crichtons; Crisp; Croziers; Cuthbert; Dacre; Davidson; Dixon; Dodd; Douglas; Dunne; Elliot; Fenwick; Forster; Graham; Gray; Hall; Hedley; Henderson; Heron; Hetherington; Hume; Irvine; Irving; Johnston; Kerr; Laidlaw; Little; Lowther; Maxwell; Milburn; Musgrove; Nixon; Noble; Ogle; Oliver; Potts; Pringle; Radcliffe; Reade; Ridley; Robson; Routledge; Rutherford; Salkeld; Scott; Selby; Shaftoe; Storey; Simpson; Tait; Taylor; Trotter; Turnbull; Wake; Watson; Wilson; Woodrington; Young.

B&B ABBREVIATIONS

As with the C2C, assume that all B&Bs are non-smoking unless otherwise stipulated. They also provide secure storage and drying facilities.

R=Rooms; S=Single; D=Double;
T=Twin; F=Family; Tpl=Triple; B=Bunks
E=**Email**; W=**Website**;
EM=Evening Meal; PL=Packed Lunch;
SP=Smoking Permitted;
DFR=Distance From Route
> = from / more than

WAY MARKING

The route is way marked with a blue direction sign complete with the word REIVERS and the route number, 10. These are posted at junctions and other strategic spots. Occasionally the road surface is signed; sometimes there are just little plastic stickers stuck to gates and lamp-posts. Signage is not always brilliant, but with sharp eyes and the use of a map you should not get lost. Having said that, sections at the beginning and end are notorious for lack of signs; vandals like to trash them, and souvenir hunters snaffle them.

WHERE TO START AND HOW TO GET THERE

A) NEWCASTLE & TYNEMOUTH

You could start your holiday by leaving your car behind – there are frequent main line inter-city trains to and from Newcastle. If at all possible, please book accommodation, meals and packed lunches in advance, and do not arrive unannounced expecting beds and meals to be available. If you have to cancel a booking, please give the proprietor as much notice as you can so that the accommodation can be re-let.

NB: Back-up vehicles are strongly advised to use main roads in order to keep the Reivers Cycle Route as traffic-free as possible.

RAIL

There are direct train services from most cities in Britain to Newcastle Central Station 0191 221 3156. It is served by **Great North Eastern Railways (GNER), Virgin Cross Country and Regional Railways**. It takes 2 hours 45 minutes from London, and 1 hour 20 minutes from Edinburgh.

To book train seats between Edinburgh and Newcastle, call: Virgin 08457 222333; GNER 08457 225225; or 08457 484950 for any other enquiries.

ROAD

Newcastle is easily accessible. The A1(M) goes through the middle of it. If you are coming by car, there is limited parking at Newcastle station, and the charge is £7 a day. There's also the 635-space Tyne Square Car Park nearby, which does special rates for five or seven day parking of around £5.50 a day 0191 243 8294. The Tourist Information Centre in Newcastle is 0191 277 8000.

AIR

Newcastle Airport is only 20 minutes from the city centre and there are regular and frequent links to many European cities, including Amsterdam, Brussels and Paris, along with international connections to the rest of the world. There are also direct flights to Aberdeen, Birmingham, Gatwick, Heathrow, Wick, Dublin and Belfast 0191 286 0966. W: www.newcastleairport.com

SEA

The International Ferry Terminal at Royal Quays is the North of England's main sea link with Scandinavia and Continental Europe and operates regular passenger services from Norway, Sweden and the Netherlands.
Fjordline 0191 296 1313
DFDS Seaways 0191 293 6262

B) WHITEHAVEN

If you choose to start at Whitehaven, the wind is more likely to be in your favour. And you will have to read Part II of this book backwards.

This Cumbrian port is accessible by train if you take the local First North Western line from Carlisle. The journey takes about an hour, following the dramatic and spectacular coastline. If opting for the train, remember to book your bike on in advance.
National Rail Enquiries: 08457 484950

First North Western: 08457 000125 (sales); 08456 001159 (customer services).

Virgin Trains (they run the west coast service): 08457 222333.

ROUTE NOTE

By Ted Liddle – originator of the Reivers

I conceived the Reivers Cycle Route in 1996 in response to several factors. The route was proving increasingly popular but because there were no other long distance rides in the region to repeat the enjoyment and challence of the C2C, cyclists had to resort to cycling the C2CV again. Variety is the spice of life and I knewthat there was a lot of superb cycling countryside in the north of England that remained largely undsicovered.

Local knowledge, some detailed map work and an appreciation of the burgeoning National Cycle Network all had a part to play in the final route selection. I decided that the RCR should be marketed as an east to west route in order to promote an alternative 'return C2C option'. The terrain, however, is in complete contrast to the C2C and offers an entirely different experience.

It was intended to appeal to both road cyclists and off-roaders; the former can tackle it from start to finish on tarmac, while the latter are offered many miles of excellent tracks and trails linked by lovely, quiet country lanes. Both options offer superb cycling which I urge you to discover for yourselves at the earliest opportunity.

This informative guide will undoubtedly help you succesfully plan your next cycling adventure - the Reivers Cycle Route!

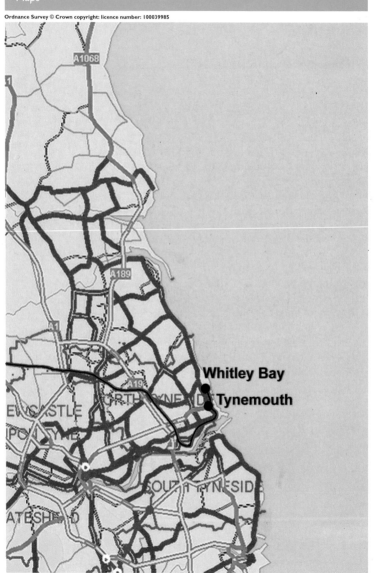

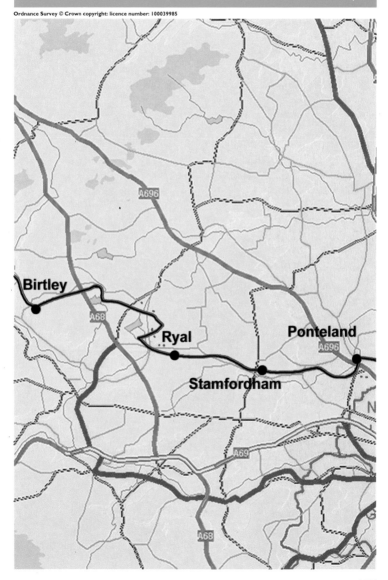

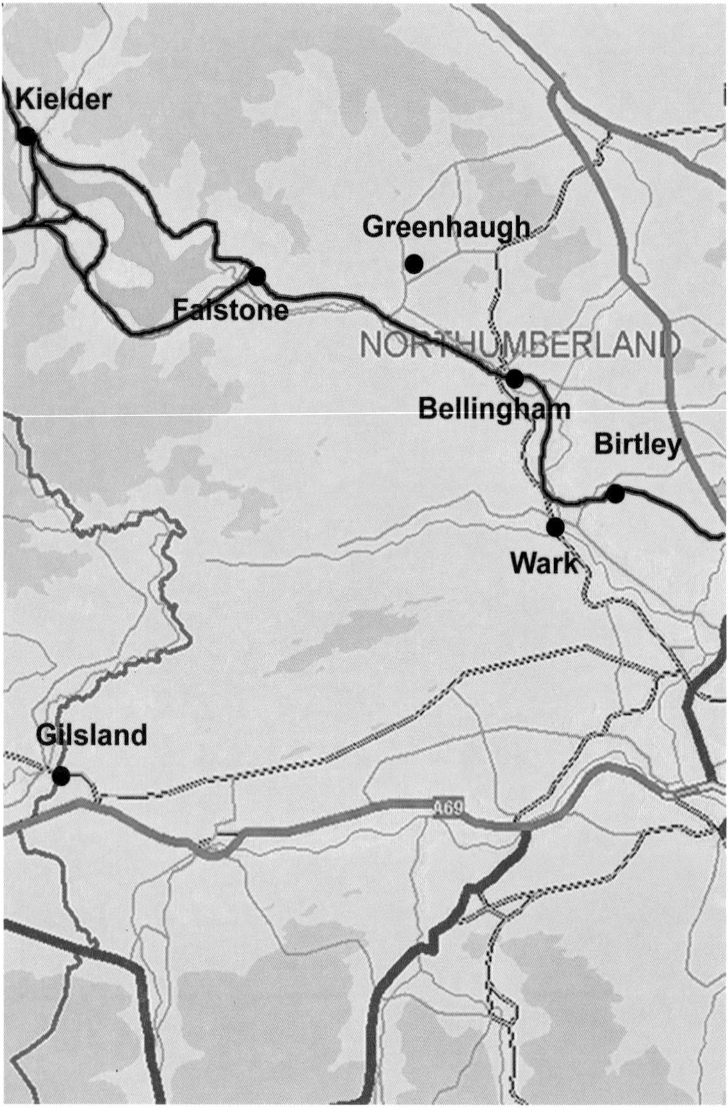
Kielder
Greenhaugh
Falstone
NORTHUMBERLAND
Bellingham
Birtley
Wark
Gilsland
A69

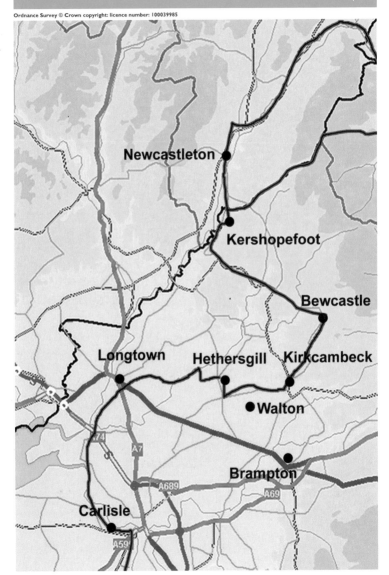

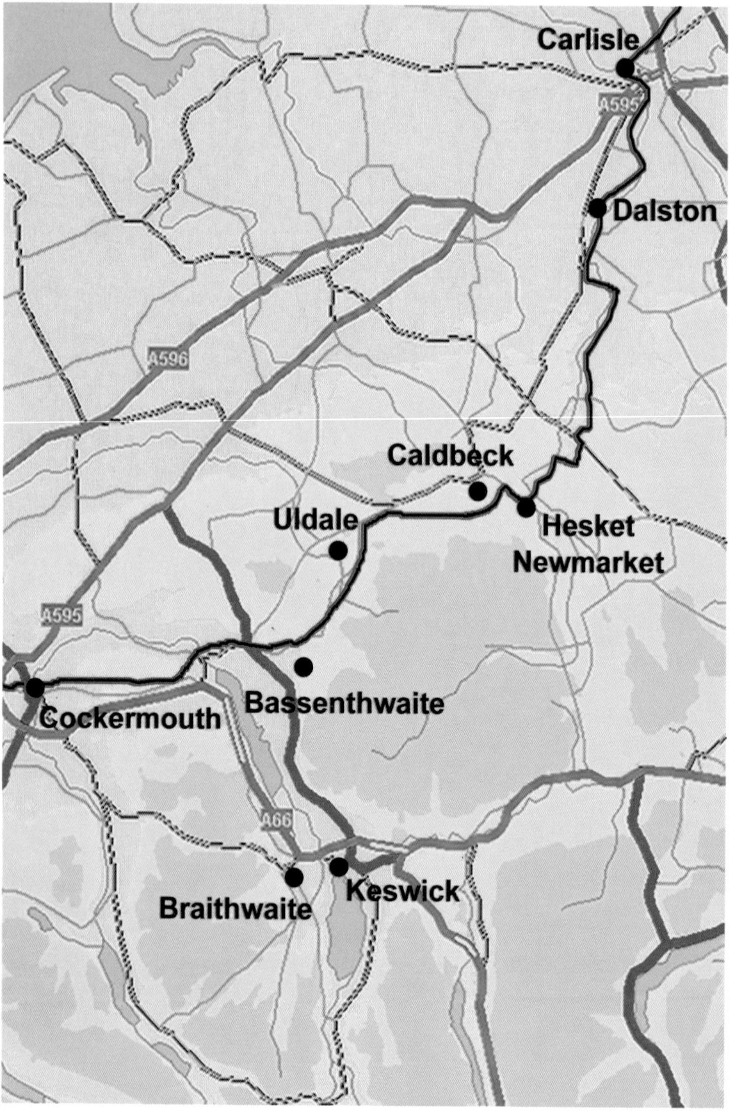
Carlisle
A595
Dalston
A596
Caldbeck
Uldale
Hesket
Newmarket
A595
Bassenthwaite
Cockermouth
A66
Braithwaite
Keswick

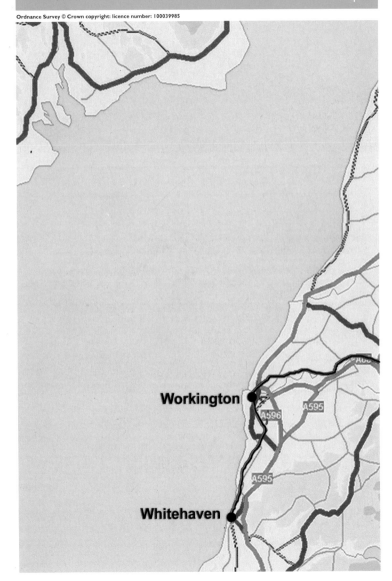

Workington

A596   A595

A595

Whitehaven

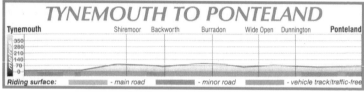

Tynemouth - Ponteland: 27km (17 miles), 18 of which are traffic-free.
Industrial heritage to Northumbrian countryside. Not much climbing.

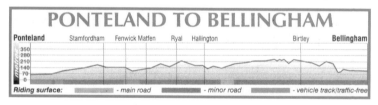

Ponteland - Bellingham: 53km (33 miles), 5km of which are traffic-free.
Into the Northumberland National Park. Some muddy off-road bits in wet
weather. Watch out.

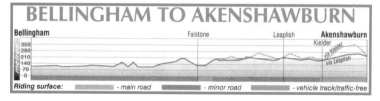

Bellingham - Akenshawburn: 37km (23 miles), of which 13 are traffic-free.
Take your choice: hard off-road, or not-so-hard tarmac alternative.

AKENSHAWBURN TO KIRKLINTON

Akenshawburn · Kershope Bridge · Bailey Mill · Bewcastle · Kirkcambeck · Hethersgill · **Kirklinton**

Riding surface: ▬ - main road ▬ - minor road ▬ - vehicle track/traffic-free

Akenshaw - Kirklinton: 51km (32 miles) of which 13 are traffic-free. Skirting the border before heading south.

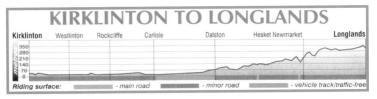

KIRKLINTON TO LONGLANDS

Kirklinton · Westlinton · Rockcliffe · Carlisle · Dalston · Hesket Newmarket · **Longlands**

Riding surface: ▬ - main road ▬ - minor road ▬ - vehicle track/traffic-free

Kirklinton - Longlands: 62.5km (39 miles) of which 8km are traffic-free. Challenging stuff at the end. Great scenery .

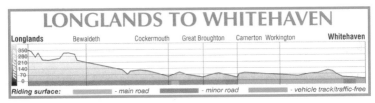

LONGLANDS TO WHITEHAVEN

Longlands · Bewaldeth · Cockermouth · Great Broughton · Camerton · Workington · **Whitehaven**

Riding surface: ▬ - main road ▬ - minor road ▬ - vehicle track/traffic-free

Longland - Whitehaven: 46km (29 miles), of which 13 are traffic-free. Skirts the northern edge of the mountains, but enjoys great views of them.

NEWCASTLE & TYNEMOUTH

Newcastle can trace its beginnings to the river-crossing and fort which we know as the start of Hadrian's Wall. Later Robert, the son of William I, built a fort in 1080 and called it Newcastle. The shipping of coal and wool played a big part in the city's growth as a merchant and trading centre, and later ship-building and engineering were to employ a large part of the community.

NB: For further notes on Newcastle and the route to Tynemouth check the end of the C2C route, which follows the same path (see pages 96-103).
See also a full list of favourite pubs, restaurants and accommodation for the city centre.

BIKE SHOPS AND REPAIRS

Jesmond: **Cycle Logical,** 37 St George's Tce, 0191 281 8383
Byker: **Edinburgh Cycle Coop,** 5-7 Union Road, 0191 265 8619
Byker: **Cycle Centre**, 250 Shields Rd, 0191 265 1472
N. Shields: **Spokes Cycle Centre**, 39 Nile St, 0191 296 2840
Whitley Bay: **Dixon's Cycles**, 184 Park View, 0191 253 2035

TYNEMOUTH - WHITLEY BAY

This charming town *(see also p.100)* owes its existence to the outcrop of hard sandstone which juts out between the Tyne and the sea defying the effects of wave and weather. Monks from the Holy Island of Lindisfarne came here in 627 and built the Priory which was one of the richest in the country and at one stage in its history monks were sent here as a reprimand for being disobedient. One poor exile wrote: "Shipwrecks are frequent and the poor people eat only a malodorous seaweed called 'slank', which they gather on the rocks, but the church is of wondrous beauty." During the Roman occupation Tynemouth was an important supply port for Hadrian's Wall. In Victorian times people flocked here on the new railway to enjoy sheltered bathing and boating.

Originally the Priory was an 11th century Norman church and is now an English Heritage site. EH also owns the fine statue to Lord Collingwood. Look out to sea and you will spot the Black Middens close to the Tyne entrance. They have claimed many a vessel, including five in three days one filthy November in 1864.

PLACES OF INTEREST

The Castle and Priory - great atmosphere
Sea Life Centre - excellent displays
Tourist Information Centre – Royal Quays 0191 200 5895

PLACES TO EAT *(see p.99)*

PLACES TO DRINK

The Turks Head, Front St., otherwise known as the Stuffed Dog because of Willie the Scottish collie, whose 130 year old taxidermised remains sit in a glass box looking at the bar. Willie came down from the Scottish Borders with a herd of sheep and a shepherd, but somehow got separated from them and spent the rest of his life waiting and pining in Tynemouth for his lost master. A tale of epic proportions told in detail on a plaque. Good Courage Directors, regular guest ales. Food served all day.

Tynemouth Lodge Hotel, Tynemouth Rd, a real locals pub frequented by the lifeboatmen. Great beers and often very busy. It's at the top of that steep climb out of the North Shields fish quays, on the edge of Tynemouth. Worth tracking back if you have got the energy.

Fitzpatricks, Front Street, is a handsome establishment. It is one of eight pubs in the small town. Has a changing selection of hand-pulled ales. Food served.

MARLBOROUGH HOTEL,
Hilary & Allen Thompson
20-21 East Parade,
Promenade, Whitley Bay, NE26 1AP
T: 0191 251 3628
F: 0191 252 5033
E: reception@marlborough-hotel.com
W: www.marlborough-hotel.com
B&B: £25 - £35. R: 4S, 6D, 2T, 4F. PL: £5. SP
4 diamonds ETC & AA. Sea front family run hotel in prime position on
Whitley Bay. High standards of hospitality and accommodation. Close to
transport links.

YORK HOUSE HOTEL,
Michael & Marissa Ruddy
106-110 Park Avenue,
Whitley Bay, NE26 1DN
T: 0191 252 8313 F: 0191 251 3953
E: reservations@yorkhousehotel.com
W: www.yorkhousehotel.com
Rooms: 5D, 2S, 3T, 3F. B&B: £27.50 - £32.50. EM: No. PL: £5.95. SP in
some areas. 4 diamonds. Near route and 100m from pub.
Delightful family run hotel. Conveniently yet quietly situated close to all
amenities. 250 metres from beach. All rooms are en-suite with fridges and
microwaves.

AVALON HOTEL,
Michael Farwell,
26-28 South Parade,
Whitley Bay, Tyne & Wear NE26 2RG
T: 0191 251 0080 F: 0191 251 0100
E: reception@avalon-hotel.freeserve.co.uk
W: www.avalon-hotel.freeserve.co.uk
B&B: £35 - £55. R: 4S, 4D, 7T, 1F. 2-star.
EM: £5.00-£10.00. PL: Yes. SP. Next door to pub. Near start/end of route.
Family run; all rooms en-suite; secure bike parking; full licence; restaurant;
new owners; washing & drying facilities.

Your Footprint map has three large scale maps, which I reproduce on with their kind permission. There is an alternative route out via Whitley Bay, but the main recommendation is as follows.

THE ROUTE

Start from the car park off Pier Rd, facing the Castle and Priory, and take the path along the estuary. Turn left into Cliffords Fort and immediately right into Union Rd where you go left through the fish quays of North Shields.

There may not be so many fishing boats now, but there are certainly a good number of high quality fish and chip shops. Union Quay becomes Bell St, then Liddle St and finally Clive St before you go right at the Chain Locker and up the cycle ramp and steps to Tennyson Tce. Follow the signs to Lowson St, going left into an alley and left onto Addison St. At the end of Lowson St go left and then right at the T-junction into Prince Regent Way. At the end of Chirton Dene Way you need to skirt round to the right of the Wet n'Wild tropical indoor water park, with its giant water chutes.

Follow the path to the right, along the cycle path parallel with Coble Dene, opposite the huge shopping centre at Royal Quays. This is where the Fjordline and DFDS ferries come in from Scandinavia, Holland and Belgium. You now cross Howdon Rd (A187). This brings you to St John's Green, off which you soon take a right turn past Percy Main Station. You will shortly be on the Waggonways, a disused railway line which passes the Stephenson Railway Museum. The famous family hailed from near Wylam, west of Newcastle on the Tyne and the museum has some fine original locomotives (0191 200 7145).

Just past Shiremoor go left over the level crossing and through Backworth, Burradon and Seaton Burn. This is where the countryside opens up, taking you past the Big Waters Nature Reserve, Dinnington and up to prosperous Ponteland, where most of the Newcastle United stars live. Once past Ponteland you are away from urban life for most of the trip.

You are unlikely to require much in Ponteland, having only covered 27km, but if you do there is a wide variety of shops here, plus pubs and restaurants. After crossing the golf course you arrive in Ponteland at the Diamond Inn. There is a coffee shop to the left and you can lunch at the pub or the Smithy Bistro immediately on your left. There is also If you are not stopping, go straight across the crossroads but look out for a sign off to the right, where you come back on yourself before taking a left hairpin through the smart housing estate of Darras Hall. At the T-junction at the end of the estate go right, then left towards Donkins House Farm before taking a track up to the right. This will take you via the back lanes to the lovely village of Stamfordham.

STAMFORDHAM

This is a handsome and planned estate village with a large green, a pond and a village green, plus a couple of proper English country pubs, the Bay Horse and the Swinburne Arms. The church may be Victorian but most of the village is stone-built and 18th century. The name Stamfordham is Old English for 'homestead by the stony ford'. It was once part-owned by Balliol College, Oxford.

Head out of the village keeping the Bay Horse on your left, passing through the hamlet of Fenwick. You will soon be in Matfen, another immaculate estate village. Here take the right turn signed for Ryal and Capheaton, followed by a right-angled left turn just out of the village. It's a couple of km until Click 'em in Farm where you first bear left then right, up to Ryal.

Just beyond Ryal South Farm there is a track off to the right: if you

CHURCH HOUSE Viv Fitzpatrick,
Church House
Stamfordham,
Northumberland NE18 0PB
T: 01661 886736
Mob: 07889 312623
R: 3T B&B: £25
EM: no. PL: £4-£5

E: bedandbreakfast@stamfordham.fsbusiness.co.uk
Pub adjacent. Pretty village green, old village pubs. 17th-c ivory painted stone house of great character on south side of green. Private residence, good breakfast, welcoming hosts.

THE BAY HORSE Gill Dempsey & Ian
Crowe, South Side, Stamfordham
Northumberland, NE18 0PB
T: 01661 886244 F: 01661 886940
E: stay@stamfordham-bay.co.uk
W: www.stamfordham-bay.co.uk
R: 1S, 4D, 1F (E-S).
B&B £33
EM: £5-£15. PL: £4
4Star, 4Diamonds.

Formerly a fortified farm, this inn dates from 1590. Serves good, locally-sourced food and fine ales and offers 21st century comfort in the heart of the village, overlooking the historic green.

fancy the off-road option, take it up to Hallington New House, where it becomes a road again leading to the cross-roads outside Hallington. Turn right. You can, of course, ignore the off-raod section, and continue to Hallington along the road.

One km outside Hallington there is another off-road option to the left, taking you across a rough farm track and over the reservoir. Be warned - the track can get pretty muddy. This takes you via Little Swinburn and back onto the main route just before Colt Reservoir.

After crossing left onto the A68 and immediately right, you will soon pass the edge of Birtley. Off to the left is Wark. You will soon come to a junction, with Heugh off to the left. Take the right fork, head to Buteland and left onto the minor road, and so steeply down to Redesmouth.

WARK

This village is about 4km from the route. It has a shop, post office, hotel and a pub. The landlord will direct you via a scenic and traffic free lane back onto the route again. Once a Norman frontier town, you enter it over a bridge. Chipchase Castle can be seen from the road. Welcome facilities in an area otherwise bereft of civilisation.

BATTLESTEADS HOTEL Bob Rowland,
Wark, Hexham, Northumberland NE48 3LS
T: 01434 230209
E: info@Battlesteads-Hotel.co.uk
W: www.Battlesteads-Hotel.co.uk
R: 1S, 4D, 7T, 2F, Disabled 4T on ground floor
B&B: £35-£45
Em: £3-£14.95. PL: £3.50 DFR: 4km (turn left at Birtley)
A converted 17th-c farmhouse carefully modernised to provide comfortable and friendly surroundings. Very used to having cyclists and will help with repairs. Close to Hadrian's Wall, a great stop-off and lovely bar.

BELLINGHAM

This ancient little market town, pronounced "Bellinjum", nestles at the foot of some of the wildest and most barren fells in Northumberland. There are medieval references to Bellingham Castle belonging to the King of Scotland's forester, but sadly no trace remains. St Cuthbert's Church is unusual with its stone roof and extremely narrow windows. Both features were included as a defence against the marauding Scots who twice burnt it to the ground. In its graveyard lies the famous "Lang Pack" grave which is associated with one of Northumberland's most notorious tales of murder, intrigue and deception. One day a peddler (a tinker, not a cyclist) came to Lee Hall, the home of a landed local gentleman and asked if he could leave his backpack there while he attended to an errand in the village. The maid said yes, and it was left in the kitchen.

She noted how big and broad the connicle shaped pack was, but thought no more about it. The gypsy failed to return that day and during the night she came down with a candle and noticed the pack had marginally moved. She ran and fetched old Richards, the wrinked retainer, who blasted it with a blunderbuss. There followed much blood and whimpering, then silence. Inside was the corpse of a criminal whose dastardly plan was to rob and murder the household in the dead of night. He got more than he baragined for. His grave lies in the churchyard, dated 1723. A plot well foiled!

There is also the St Cuthbert's Well, dedicated to the saint and a welcome addition for thirsty Pennine Way walkers, as it is right next to the pathway for Britain's most famous walk.

On the edge of the Northumberland National Park on the North Tyne river, the Bellingham area is a noted spawning ground for salmon, sea trout, brown trout and the 'Kielder' rainbow. It has two caravan sites, a campsite, youth hostel, four pubs and hotels and just about everything else including a haberdashery, gym and library. Also, it is a proper place – not (yet) a haven for second home-owners.

The annual agricultural show in the summer (last Saturday in August) is a big attraction with a country fair and Cumberland Westmorland wrestling and Northumbrian piping.

PLACES OF INTEREST

Hareshaw Linn	Superb waterfall, >1km walk
St Cuthbert's (Cuddy's) Well	Reputed to be healing water
Tourist Information Centre	Main St 01434 220616
Heritage Centre	Local history 01434 220050.

Excellent background about Reivers, Border counties railway which ran from Hexham to Bellingham and across the border. Recreation of old mine workings, plus shop of early 20-c photographer W.P. Collier.

BIKE REPAIRS Village Country Store   01434 220027

LYNDALE GUEST HOUSE, Joyce Gaskin
off Riversidewalk, Bellingham, Northumberland NE48 2AW
T/F: 01434 220361

E: ken&joy@lyndalegh.fsnet.co.uk

W: www.accommodation@lyndaleguesthouse.co.uk

R: 1S, 2D, 1T, 1suite (2 jacuzzi bathrooms)

B&B: £25-£28. PL: £3.50 Laundry.

Pub 30m. 4 Diamonds, Welcome Host Award. Relax in the sun lounge overlooking the Pennine Way. Look forward to a jacuzzi bath! And tea and biscuits in the garden after a wonderful day out in the countryside.

CROFTERS END,
Tom & Jan Forster,
The Croft, Bellingham, Northumberland NE48 2JY.
T: 01434 220034
R: 1S, 1Tpl.
B&B: £19.50
EM: no. PL: £4 by arrangement
Distance to pubs etc. 500m. Bag carrying by arrangement. Retired farming couple with years of experience doing B&B. Walkers and cyclists get a warm welcome and a hearty breakfast.

RIVERDALE HALL HOTEL, John Cocker
Bellingham, Northumberland NE48 2JT
T: 01434 220254
F: 01434 220457
E: iben@riverdalehall.demon.co.uk
W: www.riverdalehall.demon.co.uk

R: 4S, 6D, 6T, 6F, 4 suites
B&B: £33 - £49.
EM: Restaurant £15, bar £9. PL: £2.60<
SP: bar only. 2-star plus Relais Routier Gold Plate for restaurant. Country house sporting hotel, own swimming pool, sauna, salmon river, cricket field, golf opposite plus all the cycling and walking routes. Real ale in bar. Cocker's 25th year.

Chilling out at Bellingham Tourist Information Centre

The route now goes out of Bellingham following signs for Wark and Hexham. Cross the North Tyne, turn right and follow the south bank. You are now in the Northumberland National Park. Continue for about 7km to the T-junction where you go right back over the Tyne. There follows a climb into Lanehead follwed by a left. Close just beyond the remains of Tarset Castle onto the Falstone road.

FALSTONE

This secluded little hamlet lost nearly 80% of its parish under the waters of Kielder Reservoir. Today the village is a tranquil beauty spot surrounded by trees, and a good stopping place, with post office, shop and pub. A tributary to the Tyne bubbles its way through the centre of the village and, depending on the time of year, it is possible to see dippers, heron, cormorants, goosanders, and with luck you may witness the miraculous sight of salmon spawning.

PLEASE READ THE FOLLOWING ROUTE ADVICE CAREFULLY: it involves serious route choices which could either make or ruin your holiday. In the centre of Falstone take a right turn before the bridge (it is marked as a dead-end). Carry on down here for 50m and head left down a track. When you get to Hawkhope take a left at the junction and head over the dam to join the road, unless you are planning the take the forestry track along the north shore of Kielder Water. If you do, there are Reivers waymarks and also red arrows marked with the figure 6; both lead the same way. The track is good and is 8km in length, until you get to Gowanburn, where a tarmac road hives off to the left, taking you a wiggly ride to Kielder village.

You pass Kielder Castle and its visitor centre before getting to the village. Here you have another option: the sensible one, to take the right turn up past Bell's Burn bridge, Deadwater and Saughtree, then left onto the B6357 and into Newcastleton; or left and then right along Forest Enterprise Route 5c. Be warned, the latter has long, hard climbs.

If you take the south shore option at the dam, bear in mind that the road can get busy in the summer. And there is another choice to be faced: do you take the off-road Lewis Burn track to Newcastleton 3km beyond the Leaplish Waterside Park, or carry on along the aforementioned Saughtree road and head out to Newcastleton along the B6357, keeping your wheels firmly on terra firma? The latter avoids an extremely arduous off-road section through forestry, where even experienced hands have been known to get lost.

N.B. I would seriously advise anyone with panniers to take the ROAD to Newcastleton, and ignore all suggestions on the Footprint route map luring you off into the woods; it is 24km of off-road wilderness, with no services; not even a McDonalds. Newcastleton is the only beacon of civilisation (apart from accommodation around Bailey Mill) between Kielder and the village (a seeming metropolis) of Hethersgill, some 30km away.

However if you are fit and unencumbered, there is yet another tough option up Serpent Brae. This involves heading left at the Leaplish centre, going under the underpass and beetling up a severe incline before turning right and heading through the forest. You should emerge at somewhere called The Forks, where you join the Lewis Burn route to Akenshawburn, where the track crosses the border and snakes along the Scottish side of the Kershope Burn. At Kershope Bridge you can go right to Newcastleton or left to Bailey Mill *(see accommodation p.139)* and the yonder hills.

KIELDER WATER

A wild and romantic place, Kielder Water is in the heart of Border Reiver country. It is hard to imagine the cattle rustling, kidnapping and arson that flourished here in the 15th and 16th centuries. Today Kielder's stunning scenery, peace and quiet welcome all visitors. There is a wealth of facilities for the cyclist here. Northumbrian Water, who created the reservoir, has been responsible for a good deal of the inspiration behind the Reivers Cycle Route.

REIVERS REST,
Leaplish Waterside Park,
Kielder Water, Hexham NE48 1BT
T: 01434 250 312 F: 01434 250 806
E: kielderholidays@nwl.co.uk
W: www.kielder.org
or www.nwl.co.uk/kielder

R: 2 dormitories (M/F: 8 in each) + 2D, 1F.
Separate shower and washing facilities.
Bed: from £14pp.
£30 for double en-suite; £46 for family.
Discounts for groups.
B'fast additional.
EM: from £5. PL: from £5.
On route with pub nearby.
"The Reivers Bunk Room on the Reivers Route - budget accommodation in stunning lakeside and pine forest setting adjacent to excellent facilities and with a swimming pool."

Kielder: self-contained fun-centre next to northern Europe's biggest man-made lake

PLACES OF INTEREST

Tower Knowe Visitor Centre: 0870 2403549. An Information Centre with extensive gift shop and audio NNN visual exhibition. Situated on south bank very near the dam wall. Open daily 10-4/5. There is a ferry point, souvenir and fishing shop, exhibition centre, picnic area, extensive lavatory facilities, self-guided trails, a sailing club and a restaurant.

Leaplish Waterside Park: 0870 240 3549. Heated swimming pool and sauna, campsite, accommodation together with a licensed restaurant, sculpture trail, bird of prey centre, and much more. Open from April - October.

Kielder Ferry Service: 0870 240 3549. 80-seater cruiser takes you round lake - from Tower Knowe to Leaplish to Kielder Castle. Facilities on board include bar, commentary, shop, heated lounge and toilets.

Kielder Water Club: sailing club and yacht club plus a water-ski club. Watercraft hire: 01434 250217 - range of canoes, kayaks, toppers, wayfarers and dinghies.

Cycling: yes, even cycling: apart from the Reivers, there are many different routes around Kielder which might interest those of you who are doing a detour here, or perhaps meeting up with the family. Get a Cycling at Kielder brochure from Tower Knowe or Leaplish Waterside Park. Cycle hire Kielder Bikes: 01434 250392 - next to castle.

Kielder Castle: 01434 250209. Former hunting lodge of the Duke of Northumberland overlooks Kielder Village and is open daily from April to October.

KIELDER VILLAGE

At the head of the reservoir, Kielder was once a wild and uncultivated fastness, surrounded by moors and bogs. It is now a purpose-built forestry village cocooned by alpine spruce and pine trees. Before the turn of the century Kielder Castle, which stands guard over the village, would have been hidden and alone at the valley head. It was built in 1775 by the Duke of Northumberland as his hunting lodge.

Shooting parties travelled from London on the sleeper and were met at the station by pony and trap. To carry home a bag of 200 brace of grouse and blackcock in a day was not unusual. The village is a small oasis for the cyclist with a shop, pub and post office.

PLACES OF INTEREST
Kielder Castle Forest Shop, tea room, WCs
Kielder YHA 01434 250195
Kielder Castle Visitor Centre 01434 250 209
PLACES TO EAT
The Anglers Arms 01434 250 072
BIKE SHOPS
Kielder Bikes - operate rescue service 01434 250 392

NEWCASTLETON

Newcastleton, with its broad Georgian streets and open squares, was purpose designed and built from scratch by the Duke of Buccleuch in 1792. Due to the changes in agriculture there was a need for more village-based employment such as handloom weaving. The houses were built with large windows to let in light for the new cottage industries.

The town has a post office, several pubs, an antique shop , a bank, a grocery and several guest-houses. Also the garage will help with bike repairs and there is also the interesting Liddesdale Heritage Centre. If your time and energy allow, don't miss a short detour to Hermitage Castle *(see pic p. 147)*. This mysterious and magical place not only witnessed long years of turbulent border reiving, but it played host to the tragic Mary Queen of Scots when she snatched two hours' rendezvous with her lover Bothwell.

SORBIETREES, Sandy Reynolds
Newcastleton, Roxburghshire, TD9 0TL
T/F: 013873 75215
E: sandy.sorbietrees@btinternet.com
W: www.sorbietrees.co.uk
R: 2D, 1T/F. B&B £17.50-£20.
EM: by arrangement (around £7.50). PL: £3.50
Pub 2 miles (lift provided). STB 3-star;
walking/cycling award. Bike washing/drying
facilities.

A warm welcome at our lovely farmhouse with its spectacular views, log
fires, hearty Aga-cooked breakfasts & lift to the local pub for evening meal
if required.'

WOODSIDE, Michael Bogg,
North Hermitage Street,
Newcastleton,
Roxburghshire TD9 0RZ
T/F: 013873 75431
R: 1S, 2D, 2T, 2F
B&B: £18-£26.
EM: no. PL: £3.50.
Pub nearby. Red sandstone house built circa 1870 retains many original
Victorian features. All rooms are centrally heated and double glazed. Large
garden and parking for a dozen cars.

13 SOUTH HERMITAGE ST, Hazel White,
Newcastleton,
Roxburghshire,
TD9 0QN
T/F: 013873 75826
E: hazel.white@btinternet.com
R: 1D. SP: lounge. B&B: £18pp. PL: £3.50.
Pub just yards. Cosy single storey terraced cottage close to all village
facilities. Tea, coffee & TV in bedroom.

LIDDESDALE HOTEL, Denis Mckeen, 16
Douglas Sq,
Newcastleton,
Roxburghshire

TD9 0DQ
T/F: 013873 75255
R: 3D, 1T& 1F/T (E-S)
B&B: £28S occ., £50D occ
(open to negotiation).
Meals: 12-2.30; 5.15-9pm.
From £5-95 - £12. PL: £4.
Family run hotel specialising in freshly cooked food. Also fully licensed with
a secure lock-up for your bike. A handsome and solid building sitting in the
main square, you'll have a good night's rest.

THE GRAPES HOTEL, Trevor Cambridge,
16/17 Douglas Square,
Newcastleton, Roxburghshire, TD9 0QD
T: 013873 75245/75688   F: 013873 75896
E: info@the-grapes-hotel.com
W: www.the-grapes-hotel.com

R: 1S, 2D, 1T, 2F + BH
B&B: from £20
SP: bar. EM: <£4.50. PL: yes.
Family run hotel with four bars, excellent bar meals plus a restaurant. Lock-
up for bikes and drying facilities. In a lovely spot; lively or restful - it's up to
you.

Route: at the southern end of the village take a left, heading up the
hill past Sorbietrees and down to Kershope Bridge, right up the steep
hill to the telephone box and onward to Bailey Mill.

Keep your eyes peeled and follow the Route 10 signs towards
Bewcastle. You will come into Bailey and a cluster of white Buildings
which is the riding school at Bailey Mill which also does B&B, meals,
drinks. A good stopping off point, if only for a cup of tea or a pint!

Hermitage Castle - dark and ominous. Mary Queen of Scots had a two-hour tryst with Bothwell here

BAILEY MILL,
Pam Copeland,
Bailey, nr Newcastleton,
Roxburghshire, TD9 0TR.
T: 016977 48617
F: 016977 48074
R: 5T, 5D, 4F, 2S.
B&B: from £22.
SP: designated areas.
EM: <£10 for 2 courses.
PL: <£4.
E: pam@baileymill.fsnet.co.uk
w: www.holidaycottagescumbria.co.uk
w: www.ridingholidays.uk.com

Jacuzzi, sauna, public bar, restaurant: all-round comfort. A great stopping off point in one of the more remote borderland areas. Come and discover a real hidden gem.

BEWCASTLE

Background notes: the famous Bewcastle Cross *(right)* has survived 1300 years of relentless border weather in St Cuthbert's churchyard. The church and remains of the castle stand remote and almost alone save for a farmhouse in this forgotten outpost in a great sweep of wild and rugged countryside. There is a display of interpretative panels nearby in the small **Past & Present Heritage Centre.** They tell the story of the Anglo-Saxon cross. The runic inscriptions and carving are of a very high quality for this period in history.

`Summer is for grazing, but autumn is for raiding' The Reivers were far too busy tending crops and fattening the cattle in summer for plundering, but as soon as the crops were gathered and the horses fit they would be hot foot across the border to get down to the serious winter business of stealing each other's wives, girl-friends, cattle, sheep and carefully-stored winter goods again.

KIRKCAMBECK

Route: the stretch to Kircambeck is fairly straightforward. There are various accommodation choices in this area - none of them exactly on the route, but all worth a stopover to get a real flavour of the area.

WALTON

Beds in this part of the world are in short supply. To get to Walton just carry on down the B6318 - having turned left from the Bewcastle road. Walton is just under 4km and is a charming village, well worth a stopover. If you want to take a look at Hadrian's Wall you can head down the lanes to Brampton, or to Lanercost just a few km away.

Lanercost Priory, near Walton. Hadrian's Wall country

This parish lies on the north side of the river Irthing. To the east is Lanercost and to the south, Brampton. As there are neither mines nor manufacturers in the parish, the inhabitants have traditionally

TOWN HEAD FARM,
Mrs Una Armstrong,
Walton, Brampton,
Cumbria,
CA8 2DT.
T: 016977 2730
E: Armstrong_townhead@hotmail.com
W: www.town-head-farm.co.uk
R: 1D,1F. B&B: £20. PL: £4.
DFR: 4km

Pub 200m. 3 diamonds. An 18th century stone built farmhouse in the middle of the village. Provides warm, homely atmosphere and comfortable accommodation.

been dependent upon cultivation of the land. Hadrian's Wall passes through the district, and if you keep your eyes open it shouldn't be too difficult to make out traces of it in several places.

The village is ten miles from Carlisle, and like many that lie along the famous fortification, its name is characteristic, and "bears testimony to its relationship with the Roman Wall, many of the stones of which may be detected in the cottages."

THE CENTURION,
Austen & Jackie Davies,
Walton, Brampton, Cumbria CA8 2DH
T/F: 016977 2438
E: info@centurion-hadrianswall.com
W: www.centurion-hadrianswall.com
R: 3D, 1T. B&B: £24-£39.50
EM: £4.95-£12.95. PL: £5. DFR: 4km. SP: bar only. We are on Hadrian's Wall and are a traditional, family run, friendly place. Rooms are en-suite, beer garden and choice of real ales.

Austen is renowned for his food and is a wholesaler of local produce.

GREENHEAD

Not far from Walton is Greenhead, on Hadrian's Wall. Should accommodation prove scarce or should you fancy a look at some of the most interesting sections of the Roman remains then there is the YHA here or Braeside, just out of the village.

GREENHEAD YHA,
Katie Gotts, Station Rd,
Greenhead, Brampton CA8 7HG
T: 0870 770 5842. F: 0870 770 5843
E: greenhead@yha.org.uk
W: www.yha.org.uk
R: £11 per adult, £8 per child. 6 rooms available or as family or single sex multishare in this welcoming and comfortable former Methodist chapel.

BRAESIDE B&B
Bank Top, Greenhead, Brampton,
Cumbria CA8 7HA
T: 016977 47443
E: smpotts@talk21.com
W: www.braeside-banktop.co.uk
R: 1F (as D, T & Tpl). £25 or £32 as single.
Peaceful situation above the village just 5 minutes from Hadrian's Wall.

HETHERSGILL

Route: if you are not stopping in Walton or Greenhead, continue to
Hethersgill by turning left onto the B6318 (having first turned right at
Askerton Castle), then first right at Knorren Lodge.

If you are going on to **Low Luckens** or **New Pallyards**, follow
the route past Hethersgill and up to Boltonfellend where, instead
of turning left, head straight on, bearing left at the junction with the
main road. Continue across the river, taking the second left for New
Pallyards, or first right for Low Luckens. If opting for the latter, take a
further right after 500m, opposite a farm a kilometre or so up the road;
follow a metalled road up to Low Luckens. This delightful backwater
is called Roweltown.

NEW PALLYARDS, Georgina & John Elwen,
Hethersgill, Nr Carlisle, Cumbria CA6 6HZ
T/F: 01228 577 308
E: info@newpallyards.freeserve.co.uk
W: www.newpallyards.freeserve.co.uk
R: 2S, 2D, 3T, 2F + self-catering units
B&B: <£26 (£5 extra single occ.)
EM: £13.50 (set menu) PL: £4.50
DFR: 3km. Pub on site. 4 Diamonds. Farmhouse accommodation & self
catering cottages. Visit our website. Residential licence, cycles under cover,
large groups welcome. National Gold Award.

LOW LUCKENS ORGANIC RESOURCE
CENTRE,
Mike & Ruth Downham, Roweltown,
nr Hethersgill, Carlisle, CA6 6LJ.
T: 016977 48331
E: lowluckensorc@hotmail.com
W: www.lowluckensfarm.co.uk
R: 1S, 2F/group
B&B: £10-£12.
DFR: 4.5km nr Roadhead (Stapleton on the
Reivers map). Pub 2 miles.

"Based on an organic farm, we offer self-
catering hostel-type accommodation. Supplies, including organic produce
sometimes available if ordered in advance. We are 4 miles NNE of
Hethersgill grid ref NY494726 (OS Sheet 86)."
(SEE P 151 FOR FURTHER DETAILS).

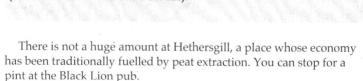

There is not a huge amount at Hethersgill, a place whose economy
has been traditionally fuelled by peat extraction. You can stop for a
pint at the Black Lion pub.

Route: From Hethersgill follow signs to Boltonfellend and head left
to **Kirklinton**. Here you are on the river Lyne, not far from Longtown.
There are lots of tiny communities dotted around here.

CLIFT HOUSE FARM,
Margaret Harrison,
Kirklinton, Carlisle, Cumbria, CA6 6DE
T/F: 01228 675 237
E: Clifthousefarm@hotmail.com
W: www.clifthousefarm.co.uk
R: 1D, 1T, 1F (E-S)
B&B: £22 - £25. PL: £4.
Pub 3km.
ETB 3 diamonds.
Spacious friendly farmhouse on the banks of the river Lyne. Beautiful walks
and fishing. Complimentary tea and home baking on arrival. Brochure
available.

LONGTOWN

This area which looks so cultivated and prosperous (putting aside
for one minute the wretched chapter of foot and mouth disease in
2001) was once so violent that there was no proper settlement outside

LYNEBANK HOUSE HOTEL,
Duncan Todhunter,
Westlinton, nr Carlisle,
Cumbria CA6 6AA
T: 01228 792 820
F: 01228 792 716
E: info@lynebank.co.uk
W: www.lynebank.co.uk
R: 3S, 6D, 2T, 2F
B&B: £22.50 - £29.50.
EM: £5-£18. PL: £4.50

Pub on site. 4 diamonds ETC. 17th century coaching house recently
renovated to 13 bedroomed hotel, restaurant and bar. All rooms en suite.
Licensed. Secure cycle parking in landscaped courtyard.

The Esk goes deep into the Scottish Borders

Carlisle until 300 years ago; that handsome bastion on Longtown's high street, the Graham Hotel, bears the name of the family who settled the town. They were also amongst the most infamous of reiving families (*see p.109-110*), whose very surname was at one stage declared illegal. That is the reason there are some 90 pele towers scattered around this area - the only way of staying alive and keeping your few head of cattle was to put them behind lock, gate and thick stone wall when the riders were abroad.

With respectability came not only the Graham Hotel, but high street banks, so if you are running low there are a couple of cash dispensers there. The quickest way to Longtown is to turn right and head up the A6071 fior 3km just beyond Kirklinton, or cross the A7 and turn right a few hundred metres past the Lynebank House Hotel. This takes you onto the Route 7 cycle way, the Lochs & Glens route which connects Carlisle with Glasgow.

Carlisle's Assembly Rooms and tourist centre: where the boulevardiers do their stuff

CARLISLE

The route from Westlinton to the city takes you down to the edge of the Solway Firth, where the rivers Eden and Esk meet and swell a progress across vast acres of mud and sand until disgorging into the Irish Sea beyond Bowness and Annan. Here you pass such erstwhile centres of shipbuilding as Rockliffe and other vestiges of a prosperous past, before cutting through a large and unattractive industrial estate. Soon, however, you are in the heart of a vibrant and welcoming city.

These days this great border city greets its guests with open arms, but not so many years ago any visitor would have been treated with suspicion. It was the nerve-centre for bitter feuds and bloody battles created by the long-running dispute over the border betwen England and Scotland. Early in its history it was an important Roman headquarters for Hadrian's Wall. In 1092 William the Conqueror's son William Rufus started to build the castle where later the unfortunate Mary Queen of Scots was incarcerated.

Carlisle Castle - a schizophrenic past

During a period of Scots occupation its ruler was one Macbeth; as 'Carluel' it was, according to legend, the domain of King Arthur, and the Emperor Hadrian was perhaps the first to realise that whoever held Carlisle could influence the destinies of both England and Scotland.

You only have to look at the vast ramparts of the castle to realise the city's strategic importance. It is the home today of the King's Own Border Regiment. If you get time, it is worth looking at its labyrinths to find the Licking Stones, prisoners carvings and the exhibition of Bonnie Prince Charlie's capture of the castle in 1745.

The cathedral is also worth a visit. The city's long-running commercial success is celebrated in the Guildhall Museum, once a meeting place of the medieval trade guilds. Carlisle's cultural renaissance and growing reputation for education have resulted in a host of art galleries, restaurants, cafés and vibey venues.

ANGUS HOTEL & ALMONDS BISTRO,
Martin & Rachel Perry,
14 Scotland Road,
Carlisle,
CA3 9DG
T: 01228 523546
F: 01228 531895
E: angus@hadrians-wall.fsnet.co.uk
W: www.angus-hotel.co.uk
R: 3S, 4D, 4T, 3F.
B&B: £26-£50.
EM: <£13. PL: £4.95

4 Diamonds. (Smoking in the lounge.) Cosy Victorian town house offering personal hospitality, superb food in Almonds Bistro/Bar Local cheeses, fresh bread, secure car parking and large cycle store. Cycle groups a speciality. (SEE AD ON P. 163)

ABBERLEY HOUSE, G. Shipp,
33 Victoria Place, Carlisle, CA1 1HP
T: 01228 521 645
E: enquiries@abberleyhouse.co.uk
W: www.abberleyhouse.co.uk
R: 3S, 2D, 2T, 1F. B&B £22.50-£25.
DFR: 2km. Pub 400m. 4 diamonds. City centre guest house, offering en-suite rooms, secure lock-up and drying facilities. Close to restaurants, pubs and shops.

FOXGLOVES, Doreen Apcar,
73 Scotland Rd,
Carlisle, CA3 9HL
T: 01228 526 365
R: 1S, 2T
B&B: £18. PL: £3.
Pub 1 minute. Lock-up/drying facilities. Family run establishment, very convenient for Sands Centre, on Hadrian's Wall route and just 5 minutes from J44of M6.

NO. I GUEST HOUSE,
Sheila Nixon,
Etterby Street, Stanwix,
Carlisle, Cumbria CA3 9JB
T: 01228 547285
R: 2S, 1T. (families welcome).
B&B £22.50. PL: £4.50
Pub nearby. 3 diamonds.
Recently refurbished. Lock-up and drying
facilities. All rooms en-suite. Near Roman

wall and city centre and within easy reach of Scotland and the Lakes.

LANGLEIGH GUEST HOUSE,
Yvette Rogers,
6 Howard Place,
Carlisle, CA1 1HR
T: 01228 530440
E: langleighhouse@aol.com
W: www.langleighhouse.co.uk
R: 1S + 3D + 3T + 1F
B&B: £25. EM: £10-£15. PL: £4.50
Pub 5 minutes. Lock-up/drying facilities. 4
diamonds.

Highly recommended by many tourists organisations, private road parking,
five minutes from city centre, welcome trays, spacious rooms. Ideal place to
stop for a final night before tackling the last stage.

COURTFIELD GUEST HOUSE,
Marjorie Dawes,
169 Warwick Road,
Carlisle CA1 1LP
T: 01228 522 767
E: mdawes@courtfieldhouse.fsnet.co.uk
R: 1S, 3D, 2T, 2F.
B&B: £22-£25. PL: £3. DFR: 2km. Pub 200m.
4 Diamonds/Silver Award. Comfortable, en-suite bedrooms, TV, tea/coffee
facilities. Ten minute walk to historic Carlisle city centre.

KENILWORTH GUEST HOUSE,
Robert & Anne Glendinning,
34 Lazonby Terrace,
Carlisle, CA1 2PZ.
T: 01228 526 179
E: loopyloz54@hotmail.com
R: 1S, 2D, 1T, 1F (E-S).
B&B: £20. PL: £3.50.
DFR: 1km. Pub 100m.
Family run business. Friendly with warm welcome. Big Cumbrian breakfast or something lighter if required. Victorian town house with comfortable en-suite rooms and open fires.

MARLBOROUGH HOUSE, Ian McKenzie Brown,
2 Marlborough Gardens,
Stanwix,
Carlisle CA3 9NW
T: 01228 512174
E: marlboroughhouse@btconnect.com
W: www.marlborough-house.co.uk
R: 3S, 4D, 4T, 4F. B&B £20-£22.50.
EM: £5-£6.50. PL: £4.50.
Pub 100m. Lock-up/drying facilities. 3 Star Victorian house situated on Hadrian's Wall within ten minutes of town centre. All the usual facilities.

HAZELDEAN GUEST HOUSE,
Susan Harper
Orton Grange,
Wigton Road,
Carlisle, Cumbria CA56LA
T: 01228 711953
E: hazeldean1@btopenworld.com
R: 1S, 2D, 1T (SP: lounge). B&B: £19-£20. EM: £7-£10. PL: £3.50.
Pub nearby. 3 diamonds. Friendly guest house, 50m from Reivers route. Large garden, secure parking for bikes and licensed for wine and beer. Complimentary therapies available - massage, reflexology and reiki.

AARON HOUSE,
Blanche Tiffin,
135 Warwick Road,
Carlisle, CA1 1LU.
T: 01228 536 728
R: 1T, 2F.
B&B: £18.50-£25.
PL: £3. SP.
DFR: 2km.
Pub nearby. Family run B&B, centrally heated, en-suite facilities available, TV and welcome tray in rooms, dinning room is non-smoking, special diets by prior arrangement.

WHITE LEA GUEST HOUSE,
Gillian Denison,
191 Warwick Road,
Carlisle CA1 1LP
T: 01228 533 139
R: 1D, 1T, 2F.
B&B £22.50-£30.
PL: £5. DFR: 2km.
Pub 100m.
3 diamonds. Victorian town house right in the town centre with all its facilities. All rooms en-suite with TV, hairdryer and welcome tray.

PLACES OF INTEREST

Tullie House Museum and Art Gallery. Excellent audio-visual interpretation of the Border Reivers 01228 534781
Carlisle Castle. Medieval dungeons, exhibitions 01228 591922
Carlisle Cathedral. Founded in 1122, fine wood carving and wall panels (office) 01228 548151

PLACES TO EAT

Number 10, Eden Mount - probably Carlisle's best eaterie. Small, popular and on route, so book well in advance. 01228 524183

Almonds Bistro, Angus Hotel - great fun, good food and reasonably priced. 01228 523546

Loaf `n Ladle, 16 Friars Court - value for money vegetarian food. 01228 596474

BIKE REPAIRS
Palace Cycle Stores, 122 Botchergate 01228 523142
Scotby Cycles, Old Bingo Hall, Church St 01228 546931

Bitts Park, from where the castle gives the town a look of that great fortified French city, Carcassonne.

Keep alert heading out of Carlisle. The new route takes you along the river Caldew from the city centre. You will have entered along Etterby St before going right down a footbpath and into Cavendish Terrace before going right again and crossing the Eden alongside the main road. At the roundabout go right, onto the subway and immediately into the park, following the signs carefully past the castle, across Castle Way/Bridge St and the railway line and so to th eside of the Caldew, keeping the river to your left.

The route is agreeably flat until Dalston, where you start heading up into the Caldbeck Fells. Various off-road sections have been built into the route at this point, avoiding the windy little lanes. The first of these hugs the river, meeting up with the tarmac option at Rose Bridge before winding down through Raughton Head, Thethwaite, Birks Hill and so to Sour Nook where you turn left onto the B5305, before quickly heading right onto the steep ascent up to Hesket Newmarket.

Eastern Fells of the Lake District National Park. These wild Fells in a miraculously untouched corner of England attracted St Mungo in the 6th century. He had heard that the unruly folk here had heard nothing of the Gospels. He came and he conquered, and many of the local churches are named after his other, formal name: St Kentigern.

HESKET NEWMARKET

Ask a local inhabitant the name of an ash tree and he will tell you it is a 'hesh'. Hesket means the place of the ash tree. Local farmers bought and sold bulls at the market cross. A pleasant village green invites travellers to rest awhile. Here you can see the Medieval stone stall where for centuries (until the late 1900s) bulls were tethered and in and around which a cattle market was held. There is a well stocked village shop, a post office, pub and a couple of guest-houses.

The Old Crown Inn serves ales brewed behind the premises, and the Hesket Newmarket microbrewery is fast gaining a reputation for

some very fine produce. Supply is limited, so sup and enjoy. This really is a perfect, unspoilt little village on the edge of some pretty wild paradise.

You are about to tackle the toughest bit of the ride with some challenging up-and-down and some majestic views. To the south west you will see the Lake District opening up, with great views of Skiddaw and the Uldale Fells.

Don't forget to stop and admire Over Water - a wee taste of things to come before you trundle down to the magnificent Bassenthwaite Lake. The rolling foothills are bunched like the shoulders of a Cumberland wrestler, full of coiled menace. Further to the east, the bonier ridge of the Pennines - all part of the C2C challenge.

DENTON HOUSE, Susan Armstrong,
Hesket-Newmarket, nr Caldbeck, Cumbria CA7 8JG
T: 016974 78415
E: dentonhnm@aol.com
R: 2D, 3T, 3F. B&B: £20-£27. EM: <£10 (pre-booked). PL: £4.
SP: designated area. On Reivers route. Pub next door Lock-up/drying
facilities. 3 diamonds. Friendly atmosphere with home cooking and log fires
awaits everyone in a large 17th century house modernised to 20th century
comforts. Comfortable en-suite rooms with tea /coffee making facilities.
Safe lock up for bikes.

Medieval centre of Hesket Newmarket, complete with tiny covered market area

GREENHILL FARM,
Arthur & Joan Todhunter,
Hesket Newmarket, CA 7 8JG.
T: 016974 78453
Splendid little campsite just 250 yards from the brewery and pub/
restaurant. Greenhill is a working farm on the edge of this unspoilt village.

NEWLANDS GRANGE, Mrs Dorothy Studholme,
Hesket Newmarket. nr Wigton, Cumbria CA7 8HP
T: 016974 78676
E: studholme_newlands@hotmail.com
R: 1S, 2D, 2T/F. B&B: £19.50-£21.50. EM: £9.50. PL: £4.
On Reivers route. Pub in village. Newlands Grange is a working farm looking
onto the Caldbeck Fells. House featuring old oak beams and open fire. Good
home-cooking and a warm welcome awaits all. Transport to local pub.'

CALDBECK

Named after the river (Cold-beck), Caldbeck was a thriving rural
industrial centre before steam-power and the Industrial Revolution.
There is still a clog-maker in the village centre. In 1800 there were
no fewer than 8 water-powered mills making bobbins, woollens and
grinding corn.

The landscape south towards to Lakes opens out. Cockermouth lies ahead and then the gentle coastal stretch to Whitehaven.

The Priests Mill, which has been beautifully restored, houses a craft centre, display area and restaurant with a picture gallery. In the churchyard is John Peel's grave , the famous Cumbrian Huntsman, and that of Mary, the Beauty of Buttermere, who was the subject of the novel 'The Maid of Buttermere' by Melvyn Bragg. Lord Bragg, incidentally, hails from nearby Wigton and is understandably proud of his local roots.

PLACES TO EAT
Priests Mill - delicious vegetarian food
Odd Fellows Arms - pub food & accommodation

2 GRAPES BARN,
Tom Reed,
Calbeck, Wigton,
Cumbria,
CA7 8DP.
T: 016974 78128
R: 2S. B&B: £25. SP.
Drying facilities. On link route to Caldbeck. Pub 650m.
Beautiful views, hearty breakfast, near shops, handy for pub, comfortable rooms and warm welcome.

Less known view, from the north west, of Skiddaw on a late autumn afternoon.

PLACES OF INTEREST
The Howk: beautiful hidden pathway through the woods to a waterfall and the aforementioned mill. Take a break and have a look...
The Clog Maker, Will Strong: next to the bridge

After Caldbeck the route winds its way round the fell, an area known locally as Back 'a Skiddaw, for obvious reasons. If you have done the C2C you will have seen the Front 'a Skiddaw.

Parkend Restaurant and The Snooty Fox at Uldale are the only watering holes for several miles, for this is gloriously open and unspoilt countryside. In my view, it is as good as anywhere on the entire C2C & Reivers route. Pointed peaks emerge from the rolling flow of hills, juxtaposing dark shadows with patches of brilliant sunshine in the autumn afternoon I was last on the route.

There are still a couple of serious up-and-downs to come but once you have got to Bewaldeth it is fairly easy riding into Workington and Whitehaven. Take your time - indeed, you will have to courtesy of the topography - through Fellside, Branthwaite and Langlands.

BASSENTHWAITE

If you are stopping off at Bassenthwaite a couple of km south of the route: just after Over Water, and the turn off to Overwater Hall, there is a left turn for this delightful and shady retreat. An alternative is to head south of Over Water, and through Orthwaite. This is part of the off-route alternative. Here you can sit outside the charming local pub, the Sun.

There is the Castle Inn Hotel just over a km away, near the shores of the lake. It has just been taken over so we have little idea what it is now like. Food and beer at the Sun is recommended. Village is typical Lake District, a clutter of whitewashed cottages in the foot of a mountain. If you are taking the off-road roud past Kilnhill and Armathwaite Hall be warned: the track can be treacherous in all but the dryest conditions.

COCKERMOUTH

There are a few ups and downs between here and Cockermouth, but nothing too serious. If you are taking your time Cockermouth is an absolute must as a stop-off *(see pages 28-31 for further details - all accommodation, places to eat and see etc. here provided on these pages).*

It lies just outside the boundary of the Lake District National Park and has long held a fascination for writers, poets and artists. It is the birthplace of William and Dorothy Wordsworth and one of the finest buildings in Cockermouth is Wordsworth House, the Lakeland poet's family home, now in the care of the National Trust.

Two other famous locals came from Eaglesfield, a mile from the town's centre, were born within two years of each other: Fletcher Christian, the man who led the mutiny on 'The Bounty' was born in 1764, and attended the same school as Wordsworth; and two years later John Dalton, who was one of the most brilliant scientists of his age, and was the originator of the atomic theory.

Cockermouth Castle was built in the 13th century, but little of that remains because of the efforts of Robert the Bruce. The majority of

Whitehaven. The end of the Reivers, beginning of the C2C. Ready to go again?

today's ruins date from 1360 to 1370.

The road from Cockermouth to Workington follows the course of the Derwent via Papcastle following the C2C in reverse, keeping the river on your left. About 4km beyond Great Broughton is Camerton. At the Black Tom climb up to the right and at the old stone bridge hang a left onto the cycle track that takes you to Workington via Seaton.

WORKINGTON

For accommodation details and where to eat etc, please see pages 24-27.

WHITEHAVEN

For accommodation details and where to eat etc, please see pages 14-19.

Congratulations on completing the 175-mile Reivers Cycle Route. Don't forget to dip your front wheel in the briny at the C2C sign!

YOUTH HOSTELS ON ROUTE

YHA Newcastle-upon-Tyne   0870 770 5972
107 Jesmond Road, Newcastle-upon-Tyne, NE2 1NJ
£8.25 (under 18s), £11.50 (adults).
YHA Once Brewed   0870 770 5980
Military Road, Bardon Mill, Hexham, Northumberland
NE47 7AN £8.25 (under 18s), £11.50 (adults).
YHA Bellingham   0870 770 5694
Woodburn Road, Bellingham, Hexham, Northumberland
NE48 2ED £6.50 (under 18s), £9.00 (adults).
Carlisle Campus (University of Northumbria)   0870 770 5752
Old Brewery Residences, Bridge Lane, Caldewgate, Carlisle CA2 5SW
(available July 15-September 13) £9.00 (under 18s) £14.00 (adults)
YHA Cockermouth   0870 770 5768
Double Mills, Cockermouth, Cumbria CA13 0DS
£6.50 (under 18s), £9.00 (adults).

CAMPING & CARAVAN SITES

BELLINGHAM
Brown Rigg	01434 220 175
Demesne Farm	01434 220 258

KIELDER
Leaplish	01434 250 278
Kielder Village	01434 250 291

NEWCASTLETON
The Lidalia Caravan/Camp	01387 375 203

LONGTOWN
High Gaitle	01228 791 819

DALSTON
Dalston Hall	01228 710 165

HESKET NEWMARKET
Greenhill, Mrs Joan Todhunter	016974 78453

BEWALDETH
North Lakes Caravan Park	017687 76510

COCKERMOUTH
Violet Bank	01900 822 169

JUBILEE ADVENTURE CENTRE

Set in the beautiful village of Crawleyside, Weardale, County Durham

COFFEE AND SNACKS

PAM WELFORD: 0191 384 9266

SLEEPING ACCOMMODATION FOR 42 - £3.50 A NIGHT

SHOWERS AND FULL FACILITIES

WELL EQUIPPED KITCHEN AND DINING ROOM - INCLUDES

CROCKERY

THE ROOKHOPE INN

Accommodation and private facilities
Quality, traditional food
Jennings cask ales
Tropical drying facilities
Magical music night, brain buster quizzes
Fully equipped cycle garage

Ring us on 01388 517 215
Email us on spottydoggy1@hotmail.com
Visit us on www.rookhope.com